# 50 Maple Madness Treat Recipes for Home

By: Kelly Johnson

# Table of Contents

- Maple Pecan Pie
- Maple Glazed Donuts
- Maple Bacon Cupcakes
- Maple Walnut Fudge
- Maple Cinnamon Rolls
- Maple Butter Tarts
- Maple Sugar Cookies
- Maple Cheesecake Bars
- Maple Candied Nuts
- Maple Ice Cream
- Maple Bread Pudding
- Maple Baked Beans
- Maple Apple Crisp
- Maple Granola Bars
- Maple Popcorn Balls
- Maple Roasted Vegetables
- Maple Glazed Ham
- Maple Bourbon Cocktails
- Maple Mustard Chicken
- Maple Breakfast Sausage
- Maple Oatmeal Pancakes
- Maple Glazed Salmon
- Maple Yogurt Parfait
- Maple Pumpkin Soup
- Maple BBQ Ribs
- Maple Sweet Potato Casserole
- Maple-Glazed Carrots
- Maple Bacon Wrapped Dates
- Maple Pecan Brittle
- Maple Bourbon Pecan Pie
- Maple Gingerbread Cookies
- Maple Almond Butter
- Maple Banana Bread
- Maple Cranberry Sauce
- Maple Sourdough Bread

- Maple Glazed Chicken Wings
- Maple Chocolate Truffles
- Maple Whipped Cream
- Maple Brie Appetizers
- Maple Pork Tenderloin
- Maple Glazed Brussels Sprouts
- Maple Caramel Corn
- Maple Mushroom Risotto
- Maple Bourbon BBQ Sauce
- Maple Apple Butter
- Maple Rum Cake
- Maple Glazed Carrot Cake
- Maple Coconut Macaroons
- Maple Espresso Brownies
- Maple Creme Brulee

**Maple Pecan Pie**

Ingredients:

- 1 (9-inch) unbaked pie crust
- 1 cup pecan halves
- 3 eggs, lightly beaten
- 1 cup maple syrup (preferably pure maple syrup)
- 1/2 cup granulated sugar
- 1/4 cup unsalted butter, melted
- 1 teaspoon vanilla extract
- 1/4 teaspoon salt

Instructions:

1. Preheat your oven to 350°F (175°C).
2. Place the pecan halves in a single layer on a baking sheet. Toast them in the preheated oven for about 8-10 minutes, stirring occasionally, until fragrant. Remove from oven and set aside.
3. In a large bowl, whisk together the eggs, maple syrup, granulated sugar, melted butter, vanilla extract, and salt until well combined.
4. Place the unbaked pie crust in a 9-inch pie dish. Arrange the toasted pecan halves evenly on the bottom of the pie crust.
5. Pour the maple syrup mixture over the pecans in the pie crust.
6. Carefully transfer the pie to the preheated oven. Bake for 45-50 minutes, or until the filling is set and slightly puffed in the center. The pie should jiggle slightly when gently shaken.
7. Remove the pie from the oven and let it cool completely on a wire rack before serving.
8. Optionally, serve with whipped cream or a scoop of vanilla ice cream.

Enjoy your delicious Maple Pecan Pie!

**Maple Glazed Donuts**

Ingredients:

*For the donuts:*

- 2 and 1/4 cups all-purpose flour
- 1/2 cup granulated sugar
- 2 teaspoons baking powder
- 1/2 teaspoon baking soda
- 1/2 teaspoon salt
- 1/2 teaspoon ground nutmeg
- 1/2 cup buttermilk
- 1/2 cup sour cream
- 2 large eggs
- 2 tablespoons unsalted butter, melted
- 1 teaspoon vanilla extract
- Vegetable oil, for frying

*For the maple glaze:*

- 1 cup powdered sugar
- 3 tablespoons pure maple syrup
- 1-2 tablespoons milk or cream
- 1/2 teaspoon vanilla extract

Instructions:

1. Make the donuts:
    - In a large bowl, whisk together the flour, sugar, baking powder, baking soda, salt, and nutmeg.
    - In another bowl, whisk together the buttermilk, sour cream, eggs, melted butter, and vanilla extract until smooth.
    - Pour the wet ingredients into the dry ingredients and stir until just combined. Do not overmix.
    - Cover the bowl with plastic wrap and chill the dough in the refrigerator for at least 1 hour (or up to 24 hours).
    - Once chilled, turn the dough out onto a lightly floured surface. Roll it out to about 1/2 inch thickness.
    - Using a donut cutter or two round cookie cutters (one larger for the outer ring, one smaller for the hole), cut out donut shapes. Gather any scraps, reroll, and cut until all the dough is used.
    - Place the cut-out donuts and donut holes on a baking sheet lined with parchment paper. Let them rest while you heat the oil.
2. Fry the donuts:

- In a large, deep skillet or Dutch oven, heat about 2 inches of vegetable oil to 350°F (175°C) over medium heat.
- Carefully add a few donuts to the hot oil, being careful not to overcrowd the pan. Fry for about 2-3 minutes per side, until golden brown and cooked through.
- Remove the donuts with a slotted spoon and place them on a wire rack lined with paper towels to drain excess oil. Allow them to cool slightly before glazing.
3. Make the maple glaze:
    - In a medium bowl, whisk together the powdered sugar, maple syrup, milk or cream, and vanilla extract until smooth. Adjust the consistency by adding more milk or powdered sugar as needed.
4. Glaze the donuts:
    - Dip each cooled donut into the maple glaze, letting any excess drip off. Return the glazed donuts to the wire rack to allow the glaze to set slightly.
5. Serve:
    - Enjoy the maple glazed donuts fresh! They are best served the day they are made.

These maple glazed donuts are sure to be a hit with family and friends. The combination of fluffy donuts and sweet maple glaze makes them irresistible!

**Maple Bacon Cupcakes**

Ingredients:

*For the cupcakes:*

- 1 and 1/2 cups all-purpose flour
- 1 and 1/2 teaspoons baking powder
- 1/2 teaspoon baking soda
- 1/4 teaspoon salt
- 1/2 cup unsalted butter, softened
- 1/2 cup granulated sugar
- 1/2 cup pure maple syrup
- 2 large eggs
- 1/2 cup buttermilk
- 1 teaspoon vanilla extract
- 6 slices of bacon, cooked until crispy and finely chopped

*For the maple buttercream frosting:*

- 1 cup unsalted butter, softened
- 3 cups powdered sugar
- 1/4 cup pure maple syrup
- 1 teaspoon vanilla extract
- Pinch of salt

*For garnish:*

- Crispy bacon pieces (optional)

Instructions:

1. Make the cupcakes:
    - Preheat your oven to 350°F (175°C). Line a muffin tin with paper liners.
    - In a medium bowl, whisk together the flour, baking powder, baking soda, and salt. Set aside.
    - In a large bowl, beat the softened butter and granulated sugar together until light and fluffy.
    - Add the maple syrup and beat until well combined.
    - Add the eggs, one at a time, beating well after each addition.
    - Mix in the buttermilk and vanilla extract until incorporated.
    - Gradually add the dry ingredients to the wet ingredients, mixing until just combined.
    - Fold in the finely chopped crispy bacon until evenly distributed throughout the batter.

- Divide the batter evenly among the prepared muffin cups, filling each about 2/3 full.
- Bake for 18-20 minutes, or until a toothpick inserted into the center comes out clean.
- Remove from the oven and transfer the cupcakes to a wire rack to cool completely before frosting.
2. Make the maple buttercream frosting:
    - In a large bowl, beat the softened butter until smooth and creamy.
    - Gradually add the powdered sugar, one cup at a time, beating well after each addition.
    - Mix in the maple syrup, vanilla extract, and a pinch of salt. Beat until light and fluffy.
3. Frost the cupcakes:
    - Once the cupcakes are completely cooled, frost them with the maple buttercream frosting using a piping bag or a knife.
    - Optionally, garnish each cupcake with a small piece of crispy bacon for added flavor and decoration.
4. Serve and enjoy:
    - Serve the maple bacon cupcakes immediately, or store them in an airtight container at room temperature for up to 3 days.

These Maple Bacon Cupcakes are a delightful blend of sweet and savory flavors that are sure to impress your friends and family!

**Maple Walnut Fudge**

Ingredients:

- 2 cups granulated sugar
- 1 cup packed light brown sugar
- 3/4 cup unsalted butter
- 2/3 cup evaporated milk
- 1 cup pure maple syrup
- 1/4 teaspoon salt
- 1 teaspoon vanilla extract
- 2 cups chopped walnuts

Instructions:

1. Prepare the pan:
    - Line an 8x8 inch square baking dish with parchment paper or aluminum foil, leaving an overhang on the sides for easy removal later. Grease the lined dish with butter or cooking spray.
2. Cook the fudge:
    - In a large, heavy-bottomed saucepan, combine the granulated sugar, brown sugar, butter, evaporated milk, maple syrup, and salt.
    - Place the saucepan over medium heat, stirring constantly, until the mixture comes to a boil.
    - Once boiling, insert a candy thermometer into the mixture and continue cooking, stirring frequently, until the temperature reaches 236°F (113°C) (soft ball stage).
3. Cool and beat the fudge:
    - Remove the saucepan from the heat and let the mixture cool for about 5 minutes.
    - Add the vanilla extract and beat the fudge vigorously with a wooden spoon or a hand mixer on medium speed until the fudge begins to thicken and lose its gloss (this can take about 5-10 minutes).
    - Quickly fold in the chopped walnuts until evenly distributed.
4. Pour and set the fudge:
    - Immediately pour the fudge mixture into the prepared baking dish, spreading it evenly with a spatula.
    - Let the fudge cool at room temperature until it is completely set, which may take 2-4 hours.
5. Cut and serve:
    - Once set, lift the fudge out of the pan using the parchment paper or foil overhang.
    - Cut the fudge into small squares using a sharp knife.
    - Store the Maple Walnut Fudge in an airtight container at room temperature for up to 1 week. You can also store it in the refrigerator for longer shelf life.

Enjoy the creamy texture and delightful flavor of this homemade Maple Walnut Fudge! It makes a wonderful gift or treat for special occasions.

**Maple Cinnamon Rolls**

Ingredients:

*For the dough:*

- 1 cup milk
- 1/4 cup unsalted butter, cut into pieces
- 3 and 1/2 cups all-purpose flour, plus more for dusting
- 1/4 cup granulated sugar
- 1/2 teaspoon salt
- 1 package (2 and 1/4 teaspoons) active dry yeast
- 1/4 cup warm water (about 110°F)
- 1 large egg

*For the filling:*

- 1/2 cup unsalted butter, softened
- 3/4 cup packed brown sugar
- 2 tablespoons ground cinnamon
- 1/4 cup pure maple syrup

*For the maple glaze:*

- 1 cup powdered sugar
- 2 tablespoons pure maple syrup
- 1-2 tablespoons milk or cream
- 1/2 teaspoon vanilla extract
- Pinch of salt

Instructions:

1. Prepare the dough:
    - In a small saucepan, heat the milk and butter over medium heat until the butter is melted. Remove from heat and let it cool until lukewarm.
    - In a large mixing bowl, combine 2 cups of flour, granulated sugar, and salt.
    - In a small bowl, dissolve the yeast in warm water. Let it sit for about 5 minutes until foamy.
    - Add the lukewarm milk mixture and the yeast mixture to the dry ingredients. Stir until well combined.
    - Add the egg and enough of the remaining flour (about 1 and 1/2 cups) to make a soft dough.
    - Turn the dough out onto a lightly floured surface and knead for about 5-7 minutes, or until smooth and elastic. Add more flour as needed to prevent sticking.

- Place the dough in a greased bowl, cover with a clean kitchen towel, and let it rise in a warm place until doubled in size, about 1 to 1.5 hours.
2. Make the filling:
    - In a small bowl, mix together the softened butter, brown sugar, cinnamon, and maple syrup until smooth and well combined.
3. Assemble the cinnamon rolls:
    - Punch down the risen dough and roll it out on a lightly floured surface into a 16x12 inch rectangle.
    - Spread the filling evenly over the dough, leaving a small border around the edges.
    - Starting from the long side, roll up the dough tightly to form a log. Pinch the seam to seal.
    - Cut the dough into 12 equal slices using a sharp knife or dental floss.
4. Bake the cinnamon rolls:
    - Place the rolls in a greased 9x13 inch baking dish. Cover with a clean kitchen towel and let them rise in a warm place for about 30 minutes, or until doubled in size.
    - Preheat your oven to 375°F (190°C).
    - Bake the cinnamon rolls for 25-30 minutes, or until golden brown.
5. Make the maple glaze:
    - In a small bowl, whisk together the powdered sugar, maple syrup, milk or cream, vanilla extract, and salt until smooth and drizzling consistency. Adjust the consistency with more powdered sugar or milk as needed.
6. Glaze and serve:
    - Remove the cinnamon rolls from the oven and let them cool slightly.
    - Drizzle the maple glaze over the warm cinnamon rolls.
    - Serve the maple cinnamon rolls warm and enjoy!

These maple cinnamon rolls are perfect for breakfast or as a special treat any time of day. The maple syrup adds a wonderful depth of flavor that complements the warm cinnamon filling and sweet glaze perfectly.

**Maple Butter Tarts**

Ingredients:

*For the pastry:*

- 1 and 1/4 cups all-purpose flour
- 1/4 teaspoon salt
- 1/2 cup cold unsalted butter, cut into cubes
- 2-3 tablespoons ice water

*For the filling:*

- 1/2 cup pure maple syrup
- 1/2 cup packed brown sugar
- 1/4 cup unsalted butter, melted
- 1 large egg
- 1 teaspoon vanilla extract
- Pinch of salt
- 1/2 cup raisins or chopped pecans (optional)

Instructions:

1. Make the pastry:
    - In a large bowl, whisk together the flour and salt.
    - Cut in the cold butter using a pastry cutter or your fingers until the mixture resembles coarse crumbs.
    - Gradually add ice water, 1 tablespoon at a time, tossing with a fork until the dough comes together when pressed.
    - Shape the dough into a disc, wrap it in plastic wrap, and refrigerate for at least 1 hour.
2. Prepare the tart shells:
    - Preheat your oven to 375°F (190°C).
    - On a lightly floured surface, roll out the chilled dough to about 1/8 inch thickness.
    - Using a round cookie cutter or glass slightly larger than your tart molds, cut out circles of dough.
    - Gently press each circle of dough into the bottom and sides of greased tart molds or a muffin tin. Trim any excess dough.
3. Make the filling:
    - In a medium bowl, whisk together the maple syrup, brown sugar, melted butter, egg, vanilla extract, and salt until smooth.
    - If using, divide the raisins or chopped pecans evenly among the tart shells.
    - Spoon the maple filling into each tart shell, filling them about 3/4 full.
4. Bake the tarts:

- Place the filled tart shells on a baking sheet and bake in the preheated oven for 15-18 minutes, or until the pastry is golden and the filling is set with a slight jiggle in the center.
- Remove from the oven and let the tarts cool in the pan for 5 minutes.
5. Serve and enjoy:
    - Carefully remove the maple butter tarts from the molds or muffin tin and transfer them to a wire rack to cool completely.
    - Serve the maple butter tarts at room temperature, optionally with a dollop of whipped cream or a sprinkle of powdered sugar.

These maple butter tarts are sweet, gooey, and utterly delicious, perfect for any dessert spread or special occasion. Enjoy the rich maple flavor in every bite!

**Maple Sugar Cookies**

Ingredients:

- 1 cup unsalted butter, softened
- 1 cup granulated sugar
- 1/2 cup pure maple syrup
- 2 large eggs
- 1 teaspoon vanilla extract
- 4 cups all-purpose flour
- 1 teaspoon baking powder
- 1/2 teaspoon baking soda
- 1/2 teaspoon salt

For rolling:

- Granulated sugar, for rolling the cookies (optional)

Instructions:

1. Preheat oven and prepare baking sheets:
    - Preheat your oven to 350°F (175°C). Line baking sheets with parchment paper or silicone baking mats.
2. Cream butter and sugars:
    - In a large bowl, cream together the softened butter and granulated sugar until light and fluffy, using a hand mixer or a stand mixer fitted with the paddle attachment.
3. Add wet ingredients:
    - Add the maple syrup, eggs, and vanilla extract to the butter-sugar mixture. Beat until well combined.
4. Combine dry ingredients:
    - In a separate bowl, whisk together the flour, baking powder, baking soda, and salt.
5. Mix dough:
    - Gradually add the dry ingredients to the wet ingredients, mixing until the dough comes together. It may be slightly sticky, but avoid overmixing.
6. Chill dough (optional):
    - If the dough is too soft to handle, cover the bowl with plastic wrap and chill it in the refrigerator for 30 minutes to 1 hour.
7. Form cookies:
    - Scoop tablespoon-sized portions of dough and roll them into balls. If desired, roll each ball in granulated sugar for added sweetness and texture.
8. Bake cookies:
    - Place the rolled cookie dough balls onto the prepared baking sheets, spacing them about 2 inches apart.

- Flatten each ball slightly with the palm of your hand or the bottom of a glass.
9. Bake:
    - Bake the cookies in the preheated oven for 10-12 minutes, or until the edges are lightly golden.
10. Cool and store:
    - Remove the cookies from the oven and let them cool on the baking sheets for a few minutes before transferring them to a wire rack to cool completely.
    - Once cooled, store the maple sugar cookies in an airtight container at room temperature. They will stay fresh for several days.

These maple sugar cookies are soft, chewy, and filled with the delicious flavor of maple syrup. They make a wonderful treat for any occasion, whether enjoyed with a cup of coffee or as a sweet snack.

**Maple Cheesecake Bars**

Ingredients:

*For the crust:*

- 1 and 1/2 cups graham cracker crumbs (about 10-12 whole graham crackers)
- 1/4 cup granulated sugar
- 1/2 cup unsalted butter, melted

*For the cheesecake filling:*

- 16 oz (2 blocks) cream cheese, softened
- 1/2 cup granulated sugar
- 2 tablespoons all-purpose flour
- 2 large eggs
- 1/2 cup pure maple syrup
- 1 teaspoon vanilla extract
- 1/4 cup sour cream

*For the maple glaze (optional):*

- 1/2 cup powdered sugar
- 2-3 tablespoons pure maple syrup

Instructions:

1. Preheat oven and prepare pan:
   - Preheat your oven to 325°F (160°C). Line an 8x8 inch baking pan with parchment paper, leaving an overhang for easy removal.
2. Make the crust:
   - In a medium bowl, combine the graham cracker crumbs, sugar, and melted butter. Mix until well combined and press the mixture evenly into the bottom of the prepared baking pan.
3. Bake the crust:
   - Bake the crust in the preheated oven for 10 minutes. Remove from the oven and set aside while you prepare the filling.
4. Make the cheesecake filling:
   - In a large bowl, beat the softened cream cheese until smooth and creamy using a hand mixer or a stand mixer with the paddle attachment.
   - Add the granulated sugar and flour, and beat until well combined.
   - Add the eggs, one at a time, mixing well after each addition.
   - Mix in the maple syrup, vanilla extract, and sour cream until the filling is smooth and creamy.
5. Assemble and bake:
   - Pour the cheesecake filling over the baked crust, spreading it into an even layer.

- Tap the pan gently on the counter to remove any air bubbles.
- Bake the cheesecake bars in the preheated oven for 30-35 minutes, or until the edges are set and the center is slightly jiggly.

6. Cool and chill:
   - Remove the pan from the oven and let the cheesecake bars cool completely at room temperature.
   - Once cooled, refrigerate the bars for at least 2-3 hours, or until completely chilled and firm.
7. Make the maple glaze (optional):
   - In a small bowl, whisk together the powdered sugar and maple syrup until smooth and drizzling consistency. Adjust the consistency with more powdered sugar or maple syrup as needed.
8. Glaze and serve:
   - Once chilled, use the parchment paper overhang to lift the cheesecake bars out of the pan and onto a cutting board.
   - Drizzle the maple glaze over the top of the bars.
   - Slice into squares and serve chilled.

These maple cheesecake bars are creamy, luscious, and filled with the wonderful flavor of maple syrup. They make a perfect dessert for any occasion and are sure to impress your family and friends!

**Maple Candied Nuts**

Ingredients:

- 2 cups nuts (such as pecans, almonds, walnuts, or a mix)
- 1/4 cup pure maple syrup
- 2 tablespoons brown sugar (optional, for extra sweetness)
- 1/2 teaspoon ground cinnamon (optional, for flavor)
- Pinch of salt

Instructions:

1. Preheat oven:
    - Preheat your oven to 325°F (160°C). Line a baking sheet with parchment paper or a silicone baking mat.
2. Prepare the nuts:
    - In a medium bowl, combine the nuts, maple syrup, brown sugar (if using), ground cinnamon (if using), and a pinch of salt. Stir until the nuts are evenly coated with the maple syrup mixture.
3. Bake the nuts:
    - Spread the coated nuts in a single layer on the prepared baking sheet.
    - Bake in the preheated oven for 15-20 minutes, stirring once halfway through, until the nuts are toasted and the maple syrup has caramelized.
4. Cool and store:
    - Remove the baking sheet from the oven and let the nuts cool completely on the baking sheet.
    - Once cooled, break apart any large clusters of nuts.
    - Store the maple candied nuts in an airtight container at room temperature for up to 2 weeks.
5. Enjoy:
    - Enjoy the maple candied nuts as a snack, or use them as a topping for salads, yogurt, oatmeal, desserts, or ice cream.

These maple candied nuts are crunchy, sweet, and bursting with maple flavor. They are easy to make and perfect for satisfying your sweet tooth or impressing guests with a homemade treat!

**Maple Ice Cream**

Ingredients:

- 1 cup pure maple syrup
- 2 cups heavy cream
- 1 cup whole milk
- 4 large egg yolks
- 1/4 teaspoon salt
- 1 teaspoon vanilla extract

Instructions:

1. Prepare the maple syrup:
    - In a small saucepan, heat the maple syrup over medium heat until it just starts to simmer. Remove from heat and set aside.
2. Make the ice cream base:
    - In a medium saucepan, combine the heavy cream and whole milk. Heat over medium heat until it reaches a gentle simmer. Do not boil.
    - In a separate bowl, whisk together the egg yolks and salt until smooth.
    - Slowly pour the hot cream mixture into the egg yolks, whisking constantly, to temper the eggs.
    - Pour the mixture back into the saucepan and cook over medium heat, stirring constantly with a wooden spoon or spatula, until the mixture thickens and coats the back of the spoon. This should take about 5-7 minutes and the temperature should reach around 170°F (77°C).
    - Remove the saucepan from heat and stir in the vanilla extract.
3. Combine the maple syrup and ice cream base:
    - Gradually pour the warm maple syrup into the ice cream base, stirring continuously until well combined.
4. Chill the mixture:
    - Cover the mixture with plastic wrap, pressing the wrap directly onto the surface of the mixture to prevent a skin from forming.
    - Refrigerate the mixture for at least 4 hours, preferably overnight, until thoroughly chilled.
5. Churn the ice cream:
    - Once chilled, pour the mixture into your ice cream maker and churn according to the manufacturer's instructions until it reaches a soft-serve consistency.
6. Freeze the ice cream:
    - Transfer the churned ice cream into a freezer-safe container. Smooth the top with a spatula, cover with parchment paper or plastic wrap pressed directly onto the surface of the ice cream, and then cover with a lid.
    - Freeze the ice cream for at least 4 hours, or until firm.
7. Serve and enjoy:

- Scoop the maple ice cream into bowls or cones and enjoy its creamy, maple-infused goodness!

This maple ice cream recipe yields a rich and flavorful treat that's perfect for maple syrup lovers. Enjoy it on its own or alongside your favorite desserts for a delightful sweet finish to any meal.

**Maple Bread Pudding**

Ingredients:

- 6 cups stale bread, cubed (French bread or brioche works well)
- 4 large eggs
- 1 cup milk
- 1 cup heavy cream
- 1/2 cup pure maple syrup
- 1/4 cup granulated sugar
- 1 teaspoon vanilla extract
- 1/2 teaspoon ground cinnamon
- 1/4 teaspoon ground nutmeg
- Pinch of salt
- Optional: 1/2 cup chopped pecans or walnuts

For the maple sauce:

- 1/2 cup unsalted butter
- 1/2 cup pure maple syrup
- 1/4 cup heavy cream

Instructions:

1. Prepare the bread:
   - Preheat your oven to 350°F (175°C). Grease a 9x13 inch baking dish.
   - Arrange the cubed stale bread in the prepared baking dish.
2. Make the custard mixture:
   - In a large bowl, whisk together the eggs, milk, heavy cream, maple syrup, granulated sugar, vanilla extract, cinnamon, nutmeg, and salt until well combined.
3. Combine with bread:
   - Pour the custard mixture over the cubed bread in the baking dish. Gently press down on the bread to ensure it absorbs the custard.
   - If using, sprinkle the chopped pecans or walnuts over the top of the bread pudding.
4. Bake:
   - Place the baking dish in the preheated oven and bake for 45-50 minutes, or until the bread pudding is set and golden brown on top.
5. Make the maple sauce:
   - In a small saucepan, melt the butter over medium heat.
   - Stir in the maple syrup and heavy cream. Cook, stirring frequently, until the mixture is heated through and slightly thickened.
6. Serve:
   - Serve the maple bread pudding warm, drizzled with the warm maple sauce.

7. Optional:
    - If desired, serve with a scoop of vanilla ice cream or a dollop of whipped cream for an extra indulgent treat.

This maple bread pudding is rich, flavorful, and perfect for a cozy dessert. It's a great way to use up leftover bread and enjoy the delicious taste of maple syrup in a comforting dish.

**Maple Baked Beans**

Ingredients:

- 1 pound (about 2 cups) dried navy beans or other small beans
- Water for soaking and cooking beans
- 1/2 pound bacon, diced
- 1 medium onion, finely chopped
- 1/2 cup pure maple syrup
- 1/4 cup molasses
- 1/4 cup brown sugar
- 1/4 cup ketchup
- 2 tablespoons Dijon mustard
- 1 tablespoon Worcestershire sauce
- 1 teaspoon salt
- 1/2 teaspoon black pepper
- 1/4 teaspoon ground cloves
- Water, as needed

Instructions:

1. Prepare the beans:
   - Rinse the dried beans thoroughly under cold water. Place them in a large bowl and cover with water. Let them soak overnight, or use the quick soak method by bringing them to a boil in a pot of water, removing from heat, covering, and letting stand for 1 hour. Drain and rinse the soaked beans.
2. Cook the beans:
   - In a large pot, cover the soaked beans with fresh water. Bring to a boil, then reduce heat to low and simmer for 45 minutes to 1 hour, or until the beans are tender but still hold their shape. Drain and set aside.
3. Preheat oven:
   - Preheat your oven to 325°F (160°C).
4. Cook the bacon and onion:
   - In a large oven-safe pot or Dutch oven, cook the diced bacon over medium heat until it starts to render fat, about 5 minutes.
   - Add the chopped onion to the bacon and cook until softened and translucent, about 5-7 minutes.
5. Combine ingredients:
   - Add the cooked beans to the pot with the bacon and onion.
   - In a small bowl, whisk together the maple syrup, molasses, brown sugar, ketchup, Dijon mustard, Worcestershire sauce, salt, pepper, and ground cloves.
   - Pour the maple syrup mixture over the beans and stir gently to combine, ensuring the beans are evenly coated with the sauce.
6. Bake the beans:
   - Cover the pot with a lid or foil and transfer it to the preheated oven.

- Bake for 2 to 2.5 hours, stirring occasionally, until the beans are tender and the sauce has thickened. If the beans become too dry during baking, add a little water, about 1/4 cup at a time.
7. Serve:
    - Remove the pot from the oven and let the maple baked beans cool slightly before serving.
    - Enjoy the maple baked beans as a side dish to grilled meats, sandwiches, or as a hearty main dish on their own.

These maple baked beans are sweet, savory, and full of comforting flavors. They are perfect for gatherings, barbecues, or any time you crave a delicious and satisfying dish.

**Maple Apple Crisp**

Ingredients:

*For the filling:*

- 6 cups apples, peeled, cored, and sliced (about 6 medium apples, such as Granny Smith or Honeycrisp)
- 1/4 cup pure maple syrup
- 1 tablespoon lemon juice
- 1 teaspoon vanilla extract
- 1/2 teaspoon ground cinnamon
- 1/4 teaspoon ground nutmeg
- 1 tablespoon cornstarch (optional, for thicker filling)

*For the crisp topping:*

- 1 cup old-fashioned rolled oats
- 1/2 cup all-purpose flour
- 1/2 cup packed brown sugar
- 1/2 teaspoon ground cinnamon
- 1/4 teaspoon salt
- 1/2 cup unsalted butter, melted
- 1/4 cup pure maple syrup

Instructions:

1. Preheat oven:
   - Preheat your oven to 350°F (175°C). Grease a 9x13 inch baking dish or a similar sized baking dish.
2. Prepare the apple filling:
   - In a large bowl, combine the sliced apples, maple syrup, lemon juice, vanilla extract, ground cinnamon, and ground nutmeg. Toss until the apples are evenly coated.
   - If you prefer a thicker filling, sprinkle the cornstarch over the apple mixture and toss again to combine.
   - Transfer the apple mixture to the prepared baking dish and spread it out evenly.
3. Make the crisp topping:
   - In another bowl, combine the rolled oats, flour, brown sugar, ground cinnamon, and salt.
   - Pour the melted butter and maple syrup over the oat mixture. Stir until well combined and crumbly.
4. Assemble and bake:
   - Sprinkle the crisp topping evenly over the apple filling in the baking dish.
5. Bake the crisp:

- Bake in the preheated oven for 40-45 minutes, or until the topping is golden brown and the apple filling is bubbly.
6. **Serve:**
    - Remove the maple apple crisp from the oven and let it cool slightly.
    - Serve warm, optionally with a scoop of vanilla ice cream or a dollop of whipped cream.

Enjoy the warm, comforting flavors of maple and apple in this delicious maple apple crisp. It's perfect for cozy evenings or special occasions, and it's sure to be a hit with family and friends!

## Maple Granola Bars

Ingredients:

- 2 cups old-fashioned rolled oats
- 1/2 cup chopped nuts (such as almonds, pecans, or walnuts)
- 1/4 cup seeds (such as pumpkin seeds or sunflower seeds)
- 1/4 cup shredded coconut (optional)
- 1/4 cup dried fruit (such as raisins, cranberries, or chopped apricots)
- 1/4 cup pure maple syrup
- 1/4 cup honey or brown rice syrup
- 1/4 cup creamy almond or peanut butter
- 1 teaspoon vanilla extract
- 1/4 teaspoon salt

Instructions:

1. Preheat oven and prepare pan:
   - Preheat your oven to 350°F (175°C). Line an 8x8 inch baking dish with parchment paper or aluminum foil, leaving some overhang for easy removal.
2. Prepare the dry ingredients:
   - In a large bowl, combine the rolled oats, chopped nuts, seeds, shredded coconut (if using), and dried fruit. Mix well to combine.
3. Make the maple syrup mixture:
   - In a small saucepan, combine the maple syrup, honey or brown rice syrup, almond or peanut butter, vanilla extract, and salt. Heat over medium-low heat, stirring constantly, until the mixture is smooth and well combined. Remove from heat.
4. Combine wet and dry ingredients:
   - Pour the warm maple syrup mixture over the dry ingredients in the bowl. Stir well until all the dry ingredients are evenly coated with the syrup mixture.
5. Press into baking dish:
   - Transfer the mixture to the prepared baking dish. Use a spatula or the back of a spoon to press the mixture firmly and evenly into the dish.
6. Bake:
   - Bake in the preheated oven for 20-25 minutes, or until the edges are golden brown.
7. Cool and slice:
   - Remove the pan from the oven and let it cool completely in the pan on a wire rack. This will allow the granola bars to firm up.
   - Once completely cool, lift the granola slab out of the pan using the overhanging parchment paper or foil. Place it on a cutting board and slice into bars of your desired size.
8. Store:

- Individually wrap the maple granola bars in parchment paper or plastic wrap to keep them fresh. Store in an airtight container at room temperature for up to a week, or refrigerate for longer storage.

These maple granola bars are perfect for a quick breakfast on the go, a wholesome snack, or a pick-me-up during outdoor activities. They're customizable with your favorite nuts, seeds, and dried fruits, making them both nutritious and delicious!

## Maple Popcorn Balls

Ingredients:

- 10 cups popped popcorn (about 1/2 cup unpopped kernels)
- 1/2 cup pure maple syrup
- 1/4 cup unsalted butter
- 1/2 cup packed brown sugar
- 1/4 teaspoon salt
- 1/2 teaspoon vanilla extract

Instructions:

1. Prepare the popcorn:
   - Pop the popcorn kernels using an air popper or stovetop method. Make sure to remove any unpopped kernels.
   - Place the popped popcorn in a large mixing bowl and set aside.
2. Make the maple syrup mixture:
   - In a medium saucepan, combine the maple syrup, unsalted butter, brown sugar, and salt.
   - Heat the mixture over medium heat, stirring constantly, until the butter is melted and the sugar is dissolved.
   - Bring the mixture to a gentle boil. Let it boil for 2-3 minutes without stirring, until it reaches the soft ball stage (about 235-240°F or 113-116°C on a candy thermometer).
3. Add vanilla extract and coat popcorn:
   - Remove the saucepan from heat and stir in the vanilla extract.
   - Immediately pour the hot maple syrup mixture over the popped popcorn in the mixing bowl.
4. Form popcorn balls:
   - Working quickly (as the mixture will be hot), use a spatula or wooden spoon to gently toss the popcorn until it is evenly coated with the maple syrup mixture.
   - Allow the mixture to cool slightly until it is cool enough to handle, but still warm.
   - Grease your hands lightly with butter or oil to prevent sticking, then scoop about 1 cup of the coated popcorn mixture and press it firmly into a ball shape. You can also use lightly greased hands to shape the balls.
   - Place each popcorn ball on a baking sheet lined with parchment paper to cool and set.
5. Cool and store:
   - Let the maple popcorn balls cool completely at room temperature until firm.
   - Once cooled and set, individually wrap each popcorn ball in plastic wrap or wax paper to store.
   - Store the maple popcorn balls in an airtight container at room temperature for up to a week.

These maple popcorn balls are a delightful blend of sweet maple flavor and crunchy popcorn texture. They make a fun treat for parties, movie nights, or any occasion where you want to enjoy a homemade sweet snack!

**Maple Roasted Vegetables**

Ingredients:

- 1 lb mixed vegetables, such as carrots, sweet potatoes, Brussels sprouts, and butternut squash, cut into bite-sized pieces
- 2 tablespoons olive oil
- 2 tablespoons pure maple syrup
- 1 teaspoon Dijon mustard
- 1/2 teaspoon salt
- 1/4 teaspoon black pepper
- Optional: fresh herbs (such as rosemary or thyme) for garnish

Instructions:

1. Preheat oven:
    - Preheat your oven to 400°F (200°C). Line a large baking sheet with parchment paper or aluminum foil for easy cleanup.
2. Prepare the vegetables:
    - In a large bowl, toss the mixed vegetables with olive oil, salt, and black pepper until well coated.
3. Make the maple syrup glaze:
    - In a small bowl, whisk together the maple syrup and Dijon mustard until smooth.
4. Coat vegetables with maple syrup glaze:
    - Drizzle the maple syrup glaze over the vegetables and toss until they are evenly coated.
5. Roast the vegetables:
    - Spread the vegetables out in a single layer on the prepared baking sheet.
    - Roast in the preheated oven for 25-30 minutes, or until the vegetables are tender and caramelized, stirring halfway through cooking.
6. Serve:
    - Remove the roasted vegetables from the oven and transfer them to a serving dish.
    - Garnish with fresh herbs, if desired, and serve warm.

These maple roasted vegetables are a perfect side dish for any meal, adding a touch of sweetness and depth of flavor that complements the natural taste of the vegetables. Enjoy them alongside roasted meats, as part of a holiday feast, or as a flavorful addition to your dinner table!

**Maple Glazed Ham**

Ingredients:

- 1 bone-in fully cooked ham (about 8-10 pounds)
- 1 cup pure maple syrup
- 1/2 cup brown sugar
- 1/4 cup Dijon mustard
- 1/4 cup apple cider vinegar
- 1/4 teaspoon ground cloves
- 1/4 teaspoon ground cinnamon
- 1/4 teaspoon ground nutmeg

Instructions:

1. Preheat oven:
   - Preheat your oven to 325°F (160°C).
2. Prepare the ham:
   - Place the fully cooked ham in a roasting pan, cut side down.
3. Make the maple glaze:
   - In a small saucepan, combine the maple syrup, brown sugar, Dijon mustard, apple cider vinegar, ground cloves, ground cinnamon, and ground nutmeg.
   - Heat the mixture over medium heat, stirring constantly, until the sugar is dissolved and the glaze is smooth.
4. Glaze the ham:
   - Pour about half of the maple glaze over the ham, using a brush or spoon to coat the entire surface evenly.
5. Bake the ham:
   - Cover the ham loosely with aluminum foil to prevent excessive browning.
   - Bake in the preheated oven for 1 to 1.5 hours, or until the internal temperature reaches 140°F (60°C) when measured with a meat thermometer, basting with the remaining glaze every 20-30 minutes.
6. Rest and serve:
   - Remove the ham from the oven and let it rest for 10-15 minutes before slicing.
   - Slice the maple glazed ham and serve warm, drizzling any remaining glaze from the pan over the slices.
7. Optional:
   - Garnish with fresh herbs or citrus slices for additional flavor and presentation.

This maple glazed ham is a perfect centerpiece for holiday dinners or special occasions. The combination of sweet maple syrup and savory ham creates a delicious balance of flavors that will be enjoyed by everyone at the table!

**Maple Bourbon Cocktails**

## Maple Bourbon Sour

Ingredients:

- 2 oz bourbon whiskey
- 1 oz fresh lemon juice
- 1/2 oz pure maple syrup
- Ice
- Lemon twist, for garnish

Instructions:

1. In a cocktail shaker, combine bourbon whiskey, fresh lemon juice, and maple syrup.
2. Fill the shaker with ice and shake vigorously for about 15-20 seconds to chill the mixture.
3. Strain the cocktail into a rocks glass filled with ice.
4. Garnish with a lemon twist.
5. Serve and enjoy!

## Maple Old Fashioned

Ingredients:

- 2 oz bourbon whiskey
- 1/4 oz pure maple syrup
- 2 dashes Angostura bitters
- Ice
- Orange twist, for garnish

Instructions:

1. In an Old Fashioned glass (or rocks glass), add the maple syrup and Angostura bitters.
2. Fill the glass with ice cubes.
3. Pour the bourbon whiskey over the ice.
4. Stir gently to combine and chill the drink.
5. Garnish with an orange twist.
6. Serve and enjoy!

These maple bourbon cocktails are perfect for bourbon enthusiasts and those who enjoy a touch of sweetness in their drinks. They're great for sipping and savoring, whether you're hosting a gathering or simply relaxing at home. Adjust the amount of maple syrup to your taste preference, as some may prefer a slightly sweeter or less sweet cocktail. Cheers!

**Maple Mustard Chicken**

Ingredients:

- 4 boneless, skinless chicken breasts
- Salt and pepper, to taste
- 2 tablespoons olive oil
- 1/4 cup pure maple syrup
- 2 tablespoons Dijon mustard
- 1 tablespoon whole grain mustard
- 2 cloves garlic, minced
- 1/2 cup chicken broth
- Fresh parsley, chopped (for garnish, optional)

Instructions:

1. Season the chicken:
    - Season the chicken breasts with salt and pepper on both sides.
2. Cook the chicken:
    - In a large skillet, heat olive oil over medium-high heat.
    - Add the chicken breasts to the skillet and cook for 5-6 minutes on each side, or until they are golden brown and cooked through. The internal temperature should reach 165°F (75°C). Remove the chicken from the skillet and set aside.
3. Make the maple mustard sauce:
    - In the same skillet, reduce the heat to medium. Add minced garlic and sauté for about 1 minute, until fragrant.
    - Add the maple syrup, Dijon mustard, and whole grain mustard to the skillet, stirring to combine.
    - Pour in the chicken broth and stir well to incorporate all the ingredients.
4. Simmer and thicken the sauce:
    - Allow the sauce to simmer for about 5 minutes, or until it has thickened slightly.
5. Combine and serve:
    - Return the chicken breasts to the skillet, turning them in the sauce to coat evenly.
    - Simmer for another 2-3 minutes to heat the chicken through and allow it to soak up the flavors of the sauce.
6. Garnish and serve:
    - Garnish with chopped fresh parsley, if desired, before serving.
7. Serve:
    - Serve the maple mustard chicken hot, spooning extra sauce over each chicken breast.

This maple mustard chicken is tender, flavorful, and perfect served over rice, quinoa, or with roasted vegetables. It's a great dish for a weeknight dinner or for entertaining guests, as it's both impressive and easy to make!

**Maple Breakfast Sausage**

Ingredients:

- 1 pound ground pork (preferably with a higher fat content for juicier sausage)
- 2 tablespoons pure maple syrup
- 1 teaspoon salt
- 1/2 teaspoon ground black pepper
- 1/2 teaspoon ground sage
- 1/2 teaspoon dried thyme
- 1/4 teaspoon crushed red pepper flakes (optional, for a bit of heat)
- 1/4 teaspoon ground nutmeg
- 1/4 teaspoon ground cloves
- 1/4 teaspoon ground cinnamon
- 1/4 teaspoon garlic powder

Instructions:

1. Combine ingredients:
   - In a large mixing bowl, combine all the ingredients: ground pork, pure maple syrup, salt, pepper, sage, thyme, red pepper flakes (if using), nutmeg, cloves, cinnamon, and garlic powder.
2. Mix thoroughly:
   - Use your hands or a spoon to mix the ingredients until everything is evenly distributed throughout the ground pork. Be careful not to overmix.
3. Form patties:
   - Divide the sausage mixture into equal portions and form into patties of your desired size and thickness. Wetting your hands lightly with water can help prevent sticking while shaping the patties.
4. Cook the sausage:
   - Heat a large skillet or frying pan over medium heat. Add a small amount of oil if your sausage is lean, but with higher fat content pork, it might not be necessary.
   - Place the sausage patties in the skillet, making sure not to overcrowd them. Cook for 3-4 minutes on each side, or until the patties are browned and cooked through, with an internal temperature of 160°F (71°C).
5. Serve:
   - Once cooked, remove the maple breakfast sausage patties from the skillet and place them on a plate lined with paper towels to absorb any excess grease.
   - Serve hot alongside your favorite breakfast dishes such as pancakes, eggs, or toast.
6. Storage:
   - Any leftover sausage patties can be stored in an airtight container in the refrigerator for up to 3 days, or frozen for longer storage. Reheat in a skillet or microwave before serving.

These homemade maple breakfast sausage patties are flavorful, slightly sweet from the maple syrup, and perfect for a hearty breakfast or brunch. Adjust the seasonings to suit your taste preferences, and enjoy the delicious flavors of homemade sausage!

**Maple Oatmeal Pancakes**

Ingredients:

- 1 cup old-fashioned oats
- 1 cup buttermilk (or milk of choice)
- 1 cup all-purpose flour
- 2 tablespoons brown sugar
- 1 teaspoon baking powder
- 1/2 teaspoon baking soda
- 1/2 teaspoon salt
- 1/2 teaspoon ground cinnamon
- 2 large eggs
- 1/4 cup pure maple syrup
- 1/4 cup unsalted butter, melted
- 1 teaspoon vanilla extract
- Additional butter or oil for cooking

Instructions:

1. Prepare the oats:
    - In a medium bowl, combine the old-fashioned oats and buttermilk. Let them soak for about 10-15 minutes to soften the oats.
2. Mix dry ingredients:
    - In a separate large bowl, whisk together the flour, brown sugar, baking powder, baking soda, salt, and ground cinnamon.
3. Combine wet ingredients:
    - To the bowl with the soaked oats and buttermilk, add the eggs, maple syrup, melted butter, and vanilla extract. Stir well to combine.
4. Combine wet and dry ingredients:
    - Pour the wet ingredients into the bowl with the dry ingredients. Stir gently until just combined. Be careful not to overmix; a few lumps in the batter are okay.
5. Let the batter rest:
    - Let the pancake batter rest for about 5-10 minutes. This allows the oats to absorb more moisture and gives the baking powder time to activate, resulting in fluffier pancakes.
6. Cook the pancakes:
    - Heat a griddle or large non-stick skillet over medium heat. Lightly grease the surface with butter or oil.
    - Pour about 1/4 cup of batter onto the hot griddle for each pancake. Cook until bubbles form on the surface of the pancake and the edges begin to look set, about 2-3 minutes.
    - Flip the pancakes and cook on the other side until golden brown, about 1-2 minutes more.
7. Serve:

- Transfer the cooked pancakes to a plate and keep them warm while you cook the remaining batter.
- Serve the maple oatmeal pancakes warm with additional maple syrup, fresh fruit, or your favorite pancake toppings.

These maple oatmeal pancakes are wholesome, flavorful, and perfect for a leisurely breakfast or brunch. The oats add texture and a subtle nutty flavor, while the maple syrup provides a touch of sweetness that complements the pancakes beautifully. Enjoy this comforting breakfast treat with your family and friends!

**Maple Glazed Salmon**

Ingredients:

- 4 salmon fillets, skin-on or skinless (about 6 oz each)
- Salt and pepper, to taste
- 1/4 cup pure maple syrup
- 2 tablespoons soy sauce (or tamari for gluten-free)
- 1 tablespoon Dijon mustard
- 1 tablespoon olive oil
- 2 cloves garlic, minced
- 1 teaspoon grated fresh ginger (optional)
- Chopped fresh parsley or green onions, for garnish (optional)
- Sesame seeds, for garnish (optional)

Instructions:

1. Preheat oven and prepare salmon:
    - Preheat your oven to 400°F (200°C). Line a baking sheet with parchment paper or foil for easy cleanup.
    - Pat the salmon fillets dry with paper towels. Season both sides with salt and pepper.
2. Make the maple glaze:
    - In a small bowl, whisk together the maple syrup, soy sauce, Dijon mustard,
    - minced garlic, and grated ginger (if using).
3. Glaze the salmon:
    - Place the salmon fillets on the prepared baking sheet, evenly spaced apart.
    - Brush the maple glaze over the tops of the salmon fillets, using a pastry brush or spoon to coat them generously.
4. Bake the salmon:
    - Bake in the preheated oven for 12-15 minutes, or until the salmon is cooked through and flakes easily with a fork. The internal temperature should reach 145°F (63°C).
5. Broil (optional):
    - If desired, you can broil the salmon for an additional 1-2 minutes after baking to caramelize the glaze slightly and give the salmon a nice browned finish. Watch carefully to prevent burning.
6. Serve:
    - Remove the maple glazed salmon from the oven and transfer to serving plates.
    - Garnish with chopped fresh parsley or green onions, and sprinkle with sesame seeds if desired.
7. Serve and enjoy:
    - Serve the maple glazed salmon hot, accompanied by your favorite side dishes such as rice, quinoa, or roasted vegetables.

This maple glazed salmon is tender, flavorful, and perfect for a quick and easy weeknight dinner or for entertaining guests. The combination of sweet maple syrup and savory soy sauce complements the richness of the salmon beautifully, creating a dish that is sure to impress!

**Maple Yogurt Parfait**

Ingredients:

- 1 cup plain Greek yogurt (or yogurt of your choice)
- 2 tablespoons pure maple syrup
- 1/2 cup granola
- 1 cup mixed berries (such as strawberries, blueberries, raspberries)
- Optional toppings: sliced bananas, chopped nuts, chia seeds, shredded coconut

Instructions:

1. Prepare the yogurt:
    - In a small bowl, mix together the plain Greek yogurt and pure maple syrup until well combined. Adjust the amount of maple syrup to your taste preference for sweetness.
2. Assemble the parfait:
    - Start by layering the maple yogurt, granola, and mixed berries in a glass or a bowl. Repeat the layers until you've used up all the ingredients or reached the desired amount.
3. Add optional toppings:
    - If desired, sprinkle sliced bananas, chopped nuts, chia seeds, or shredded coconut on top of the parfait for added texture and flavor.
4. Serve:
    - Serve the maple yogurt parfait immediately as a satisfying breakfast or snack option.
5. Variations:
    - You can customize your maple yogurt parfait with different fruits, such as mango, pineapple, or kiwi.
    - Use flavored yogurt, such as vanilla or honey yogurt, for additional sweetness.
    - Substitute the granola with crushed nuts, oats, or your favorite breakfast cereal for a different texture.

This maple yogurt parfait is not only delicious but also packed with protein, fiber, and vitamins from the yogurt and fresh fruits. It's a versatile dish that can be enjoyed year-round and is perfect for starting your day off right or as a refreshing snack. Enjoy!

**Maple Pumpkin Soup**

Ingredients:

- 1 tablespoon olive oil
- 1 onion, chopped
- 2 cloves garlic, minced
- 1 teaspoon ground cumin
- 1/2 teaspoon ground cinnamon
- 1/4 teaspoon ground nutmeg
- 1/4 teaspoon ground ginger
- 1/4 teaspoon ground cloves
- 1/4 teaspoon cayenne pepper (optional, for heat)
- 4 cups pumpkin puree (canned or homemade)
- 4 cups vegetable broth (or chicken broth)
- 1/2 cup pure maple syrup
- Salt and pepper, to taste
- 1/2 cup heavy cream or coconut milk (optional, for creaminess)
- Toasted pumpkin seeds, for garnish (optional)
- Fresh herbs (such as parsley or cilantro), for garnish (optional)

Instructions:

1. Sauté aromatics:
   - In a large pot or Dutch oven, heat olive oil over medium heat. Add chopped onion and sauté until translucent, about 5 minutes.
   - Add minced garlic, ground cumin, ground cinnamon, ground nutmeg, ground ginger, ground cloves, and cayenne pepper (if using). Sauté for another 1-2 minutes until fragrant.
2. Add pumpkin and broth:
   - Stir in the pumpkin puree and vegetable broth. Bring the mixture to a simmer.
3. Simmer and season:
   - Reduce heat to low and let the soup simmer for about 15-20 minutes, stirring occasionally, to allow the flavors to meld together.
   - Season with salt and pepper to taste.
4. Add maple syrup:
   - Stir in the pure maple syrup, adjusting the amount to your desired level of sweetness.
5. Blend the soup:
   - Remove the soup from heat. Use an immersion blender to puree the soup until smooth and creamy. Alternatively, carefully transfer the soup in batches to a blender and blend until smooth, then return it to the pot.
6. Add cream (optional):
   - If using, stir in the heavy cream or coconut milk to add richness to the soup. Heat through gently over low heat, if needed.

7. Serve:
    - Ladle the maple pumpkin soup into bowls. Garnish with toasted pumpkin seeds and fresh herbs, if desired.
8. Enjoy:
    - Serve the maple pumpkin soup hot, alongside crusty bread or a salad for a complete meal.

This maple pumpkin soup is perfect for autumn or winter meals, offering a blend of seasonal flavors that are both comforting and nutritious. The addition of maple syrup adds a delightful sweetness that complements the savory spices and creamy texture of the soup. It's sure to be a hit at any dinner table!

**Maple BBQ Ribs**

Ingredients:

- 2 racks of pork ribs (about 4-5 pounds total)
- Salt and pepper, to taste
- 1 cup barbecue sauce (your favorite store-bought or homemade)
- 1/2 cup pure maple syrup
- 1/4 cup apple cider vinegar
- 2 tablespoons Dijon mustard
- 2 cloves garlic, minced
- 1 teaspoon smoked paprika
- 1/2 teaspoon ground cumin
- 1/2 teaspoon ground cinnamon
- 1/4 teaspoon cayenne pepper (optional, for heat)

Instructions:

1. Prepare the ribs:
    - Remove the membrane from the back of the ribs (if not already done). Season both sides of the ribs generously with salt and pepper.
2. Make the maple BBQ sauce:
    - In a medium bowl, whisk together barbecue sauce, pure maple syrup, apple cider vinegar, Dijon mustard, minced garlic, smoked paprika, ground cumin, ground cinnamon, and cayenne pepper (if using).
3. Prepare the ribs for cooking:
    - If using a grill: Preheat your grill to medium-high heat (about 350-400°F / 175-200°C). If using an oven: Preheat your oven to 300°F (150°C).
4. Cook the ribs:
    - Grilling method: Place the seasoned ribs directly on the grill. Grill for about 20-30 minutes per side, brushing generously with the maple BBQ sauce during the last 10-15 minutes of cooking. Cook until the ribs are tender and cooked through, with an internal temperature of 190°F (88°C).
    - Oven method: Place the seasoned ribs on a foil-lined baking sheet. Cover tightly with aluminum foil. Bake in the preheated oven for 2.5-3 hours, or until the ribs are tender and nearly falling off the bone. Remove the foil and brush the ribs generously with the maple BBQ sauce. Increase the oven temperature to 400°F (200°C) and bake for an additional 15-20 minutes, or until the sauce is sticky and caramelized.
5. Serve:
    - Remove the maple BBQ ribs from the grill or oven and let them rest for a few minutes.
    - Slice the ribs between the bones and serve hot, drizzling any remaining sauce over the top.
6. Enjoy:

- Serve the maple BBQ ribs with your favorite sides, such as coleslaw, cornbread, or grilled vegetables.

These maple BBQ ribs are sure to be a hit at your next barbecue or gathering. The combination of sweet maple syrup and tangy barbecue sauce creates a sticky glaze that enhances the natural flavors of the tender ribs. Enjoy the deliciousness!

**Maple Sweet Potato Casserole**

Ingredients:

For the sweet potato filling:

- 3 lbs sweet potatoes (about 4 medium sweet potatoes), peeled and cubed
- 1/2 cup unsalted butter, melted
- 1/2 cup pure maple syrup
- 1/4 cup milk (or cream, for richer texture)
- 2 large eggs, beaten
- 1 teaspoon vanilla extract
- 1/2 teaspoon ground cinnamon
- 1/4 teaspoon ground nutmeg
- 1/4 teaspoon salt

For the pecan streusel topping:

- 1 cup pecans, chopped
- 1/2 cup brown sugar, packed
- 1/4 cup all-purpose flour
- 1/4 cup unsalted butter, melted

Instructions:

1. Prepare the sweet potatoes:
   - Peel the sweet potatoes and cut them into evenly sized cubes.
   - Place the sweet potato cubes in a large pot and cover with water. Bring to a boil over medium-high heat, then reduce the heat to medium-low and simmer for about 15-20 minutes, or until the sweet potatoes are tender when pierced with a fork.
   - Drain the sweet potatoes and transfer them to a large mixing bowl.
2. Make the sweet potato filling:
   - Preheat your oven to 350°F (175°C).
   - Mash the cooked sweet potatoes with a potato masher until smooth.
   - Add melted butter, pure maple syrup, milk (or cream), beaten eggs, vanilla extract, ground cinnamon, ground nutmeg, and salt to the mashed sweet potatoes. Stir until well combined and smooth.
3. Prepare the pecan streusel topping:
   - In a separate bowl, combine chopped pecans, brown sugar, all-purpose flour, and melted butter. Mix until crumbly and well combined.
4. Assemble the casserole:
   - Transfer the sweet potato mixture to a lightly greased 9x13-inch baking dish, spreading it out evenly.
   - Sprinkle the pecan streusel topping evenly over the sweet potato mixture.

5. Bake the casserole:
    - Bake in the preheated oven for 25-30 minutes, or until the pecan streusel topping is golden brown and crisp.
6. Serve:
    - Remove the maple sweet potato casserole from the oven and let it cool for a few minutes before serving.
    - Serve warm as a side dish for Thanksgiving dinner or any festive meal.

This maple sweet potato casserole is a perfect balance of creamy, sweet, and crunchy textures, making it a favorite dish for holiday gatherings or any time you crave a comforting and satisfying side dish. Enjoy the delicious flavors of maple syrup and sweet potatoes in every bite!

**Maple-Glazed Carrots**

Ingredients:

- 1 pound carrots, peeled and sliced diagonally into 1/4-inch thick slices
- 2 tablespoons unsalted butter
- 2 tablespoons pure maple syrup
- Salt and pepper, to taste
- Fresh parsley, chopped (for garnish, optional)

Instructions:

1. Cook the carrots:
    - In a large skillet or saucepan, melt the butter over medium heat.
    - Add the sliced carrots to the skillet and sauté for 3-4 minutes, stirring occasionally, until the carrots start to soften slightly.
2. Glaze the carrots:
    - Drizzle the maple syrup over the carrots in the skillet.
    - Stir well to coat the carrots evenly with the maple syrup and butter mixture.
3. Simmer and cook:
    - Reduce the heat to medium-low and cover the skillet. Let the carrots simmer for 8-10 minutes, or until the carrots are tender and glazed, stirring occasionally.
4. Season and garnish:
    - Season the maple-glazed carrots with salt and pepper to taste.
    - If desired, garnish with chopped fresh parsley for added color and flavor.
5. Serve:
    - Transfer the maple-glazed carrots to a serving dish and serve hot as a side dish.

These maple-glazed carrots are a wonderful addition to any meal, whether it's a holiday feast or a simple weeknight dinner. The maple syrup adds a delightful sweetness that complements the natural sweetness of the carrots, making them both delicious and kid-friendly. Enjoy these flavorful glazed carrots as a perfect accompaniment to your favorite main dishes!

**Maple Bacon Wrapped Dates**

Ingredients:

- 16 Medjool dates, pitted
- 8 slices of bacon, cut in half crosswise (you'll have 16 pieces)
- 1/4 cup pure maple syrup
- Toothpicks or wooden skewers

Instructions:

1. Preheat oven:
    - Preheat your oven to 375°F (190°C). Line a baking sheet with parchment paper or aluminum foil for easy cleanup.
2. Prepare the dates:
    - Make a small slit in each date and remove the pits.
3. Wrap with bacon:
    - Take a piece of bacon and wrap it around a date, securing it with a toothpick or wooden skewer. Repeat with the remaining dates and bacon pieces.
4. Glaze with maple syrup:
    - Arrange the bacon-wrapped dates on the prepared baking sheet.
    - Brush or drizzle each date generously with pure maple syrup.
5. Bake:
    - Bake in the preheated oven for 15-20 minutes, or until the bacon is crispy and cooked through, and the dates are caramelized.
6. Serve:
    - Remove the maple bacon-wrapped dates from the oven and let them cool for a few minutes before serving.
    - Serve warm as an appetizer or party snack. Optionally, you can remove the toothpicks or skewers before serving.

These maple bacon-wrapped dates are a crowd-pleasing appetizer with a perfect balance of sweet and salty flavors. They are great for entertaining, as they can be prepared ahead of time and baked just before serving. Enjoy these delightful bites of goodness at your next gathering!

**Maple Pecan Brittle**

Ingredients:

- 1 cup granulated sugar
- 1/2 cup pure maple syrup
- 1/4 cup water
- 1/2 cup unsalted butter, cut into pieces
- 1/4 teaspoon salt
- 1 cup pecans, chopped
- 1 teaspoon vanilla extract
- 1/2 teaspoon baking soda

Instructions:

1. Prepare the baking sheet:
    - Line a baking sheet with parchment paper or a silicone baking mat. Set aside.
2. Cook the sugar mixture:
    - In a heavy-bottomed saucepan, combine the granulated sugar, maple syrup, and water over medium-high heat. Stir until the sugar dissolves.
    - Once the mixture comes to a boil, stop stirring and insert a candy thermometer. Cook the mixture until it reaches 300°F (hard crack stage). This will take about 10-15 minutes.
3. Add butter and pecans:
    - Carefully stir in the butter, chopped pecans, and salt. The mixture will bubble vigorously.
4. Finish the brittle:
    - Continue cooking, stirring constantly, until the mixture reaches 280°F again (soft crack stage).
    - Remove the saucepan from heat and quickly stir in the vanilla extract and baking soda. The mixture will foam up.
5. Spread the brittle:
    - Immediately pour the hot mixture onto the prepared baking sheet. Use a spatula or wooden spoon to spread it out into an even layer, about 1/4 inch thick.
6. Cool and break into pieces:
    - Let the maple pecan brittle cool completely at room temperature until hardened, about 30 minutes to 1 hour.
    - Once cooled and hardened, break the brittle into pieces using your hands or a kitchen mallet.
7. Store the brittle:
    - Store the maple pecan brittle in an airtight container at room temperature. It will keep well for up to 2 weeks.
8. Enjoy:
    - Serve the maple pecan brittle as a sweet treat or gift it to friends and family during holidays or special occasions.

This maple pecan brittle recipe yields a crunchy and delicious confection with the distinctive flavors of maple syrup and pecans. It's perfect for satisfying your sweet tooth or for giving as a homemade gift. Enjoy the delightful crunch and sweetness of this maple pecan brittle!

**Maple Bourbon Pecan Pie**

Ingredients:

- 1 pie crust (store-bought or homemade)
- 1 cup pecan halves
- 3 large eggs
- 1 cup pure maple syrup
- 1/4 cup bourbon
- 1/2 cup packed light brown sugar
- 4 tablespoons unsalted butter, melted
- 1 teaspoon vanilla extract
- 1/4 teaspoon salt

Instructions:

1. Preheat oven:
    - Preheat your oven to 350°F (175°C). Place the pie crust in a 9-inch pie dish and set aside.
2. Toast pecans (optional):
    - Spread the pecan halves on a baking sheet and toast them in the preheated oven for 8-10 minutes, or until fragrant. Remove from the oven and let them cool slightly.
3. Prepare the filling:
    - In a large mixing bowl, whisk together the eggs, pure maple syrup, bourbon, light brown sugar, melted butter, vanilla extract, and salt until well combined.
4. Assemble the pie:
    - Arrange the toasted pecan halves evenly in the bottom of the prepared pie crust.
    - Pour the maple bourbon filling mixture over the pecans.
5. Bake the pie:
    - Place the pie on a baking sheet (to catch any potential spills) and bake in the preheated oven for 45-50 minutes, or until the pie is set and the center is slightly jiggly but not liquid.
    - If the crust starts to brown too quickly, cover the edges with foil or a pie crust shield halfway through baking.
6. Cool and serve:
    - Remove the maple bourbon pecan pie from the oven and let it cool completely on a wire rack before serving.
    - Serve slices of the pie at room temperature or slightly warmed, optionally with a scoop of vanilla ice cream or a dollop of whipped cream.
7. Enjoy:
    - Enjoy this delicious maple bourbon pecan pie as a decadent dessert, perfect for holidays or special occasions.

This maple bourbon pecan pie is rich, sweet, and has a delightful depth of flavor from the combination of maple syrup and bourbon. It's sure to be a hit with pecan pie lovers and anyone who enjoys a touch of bourbon in their desserts!

**Maple Gingerbread Cookies**

Ingredients:

- 3 cups all-purpose flour
- 1 teaspoon baking soda
- 1/2 teaspoon salt
- 1 tablespoon ground ginger
- 1 teaspoon ground cinnamon
- 1/4 teaspoon ground cloves
- 1/4 teaspoon ground nutmeg
- 1/2 cup unsalted butter, softened
- 1/2 cup packed brown sugar
- 1/2 cup pure maple syrup
- 1 large egg
- 1 teaspoon vanilla extract
- Additional flour for rolling out the dough

Instructions:

1. Preheat oven:
    - Preheat your oven to 350°F (175°C). Line baking sheets with parchment paper or silicone baking mats.
2. Prepare dry ingredients:
    - In a medium bowl, whisk together the flour, baking soda, salt, ground ginger, ground cinnamon, ground cloves, and ground nutmeg. Set aside.
3. Cream butter and sugar:
    - In a large bowl or the bowl of a stand mixer, beat together the softened butter and brown sugar until light and fluffy.
4. Add wet ingredients:
    - Add the pure maple syrup, egg, and vanilla extract to the butter-sugar mixture. Beat until well combined.
5. Combine dry and wet ingredients:
    - Gradually add the dry ingredients to the wet ingredients, mixing until a dough forms. If the dough is too sticky, add a little more flour, 1 tablespoon at a time, until it is easy to handle.
6. Chill the dough (optional):
    - Wrap the dough in plastic wrap and chill in the refrigerator for at least 1 hour, or until firm. Chilling the dough will make it easier to roll out and cut into shapes.
7. Roll out and cut cookies:
    - On a lightly floured surface, roll out the chilled dough to about 1/4-inch thickness.
    - Use cookie cutters to cut out desired shapes. Place the cut-out cookies onto the prepared baking sheets, spacing them about 1 inch apart.
8. Bake the cookies:

- Bake in the preheated oven for 8-10 minutes, or until the edges are lightly browned.
9. Cool and decorate:
    - Remove the cookies from the oven and let them cool on the baking sheets for a few minutes before transferring them to a wire rack to cool completely.
    - Once cooled, decorate the maple gingerbread cookies with royal icing, if desired, or simply enjoy them plain.
10. Enjoy:
    - Serve and enjoy these delicious maple gingerbread cookies with a cup of hot cocoa or your favorite festive drink!

These maple gingerbread cookies are perfect for the holiday season or any time you crave a cozy, spiced treat. The addition of maple syrup adds a lovely sweetness that complements the warm spices beautifully. Enjoy baking and sharing these delightful cookies with family and friends!

**Maple Almond Butter**

Ingredients:

- 2 cups raw almonds
- 2-3 tablespoons pure maple syrup (adjust to taste)
- 1/2 teaspoon vanilla extract
- 1/4 teaspoon salt (optional)

Instructions:

1. Roast the almonds:
    - Preheat your oven to 350°F (175°C).
    - Spread the almonds evenly on a baking sheet.
    - Roast the almonds in the preheated oven for 10-12 minutes, stirring halfway through, until they are fragrant and lightly golden. Be careful not to let them burn.
2. Cool the almonds:
    - Remove the almonds from the oven and let them cool for a few minutes until they are comfortable to handle.
3. Make almond butter:
    - Transfer the roasted almonds to a food processor or high-speed blender.
    - Process the almonds, scraping down the sides as needed, until they form a smooth and creamy almond butter consistency. This process can take 10-15 minutes depending on your appliance.
4. Add maple syrup and vanilla:
    - Once the almond butter is smooth, add 2 tablespoons of maple syrup, vanilla extract, and salt (if using).
    - Process again until everything is well combined and the almond butter reaches your desired sweetness and consistency. Taste and add more maple syrup if you prefer a sweeter flavor.
5. Store:
    - Transfer the maple almond butter to a clean jar or airtight container.
    - Store in the refrigerator for up to 2 weeks. Stir before using as natural oils may separate and rise to the top.
6. Enjoy:
    - Serve your homemade maple almond butter on toast, drizzle it over oatmeal, use it as a dip for apple slices, or enjoy it straight from the jar!

Homemade maple almond butter is a healthier alternative to store-bought varieties and allows you to control the sweetness and ingredients. It's packed with protein, healthy fats, and a delightful maple flavor that makes it a versatile and delicious addition to your pantry.

**Maple Banana Bread**

Ingredients:

- 3 ripe bananas, mashed
- 1/2 cup unsalted butter, melted
- 1/2 cup pure maple syrup
- 2 large eggs
- 1 teaspoon vanilla extract
- 1 3/4 cups all-purpose flour
- 1 teaspoon baking soda
- 1/2 teaspoon baking powder
- 1/2 teaspoon salt
- 1/2 teaspoon ground cinnamon (optional)
- 1/2 cup chopped walnuts or pecans (optional)

Instructions:

1. Preheat oven:
    - Preheat your oven to 350°F (175°C). Grease a 9x5-inch loaf pan or line it with parchment paper for easy removal.
2. Prepare wet ingredients:
    - In a large mixing bowl, mash the ripe bananas with a fork or potato masher until smooth.
    - Add melted butter and pure maple syrup to the mashed bananas. Stir until well combined.
    - Add the eggs and vanilla extract to the banana mixture. Mix well.
3. Combine dry ingredients:
    - In a separate bowl, whisk together the flour, baking soda, baking powder, salt, and ground cinnamon (if using).
4. Mix batter:
    - Gradually add the dry ingredients to the wet ingredients, mixing until just combined. Be careful not to overmix.
    - If using, gently fold in chopped walnuts or pecans into the batter.
5. Bake the banana bread:
    - Pour the batter into the prepared loaf pan, spreading it out evenly.
    - Bake in the preheated oven for 50-60 minutes, or until a toothpick inserted into the center comes out clean or with a few moist crumbs.
6. Cool and serve:
    - Remove the banana bread from the oven and let it cool in the pan for 10-15 minutes.
    - Carefully transfer the banana bread to a wire rack to cool completely before slicing.
7. Enjoy:

- Slice the maple banana bread and serve it warm or at room temperature. Enjoy plain, with a smear of butter, or with a drizzle of maple syrup.

This maple banana bread is perfect for breakfast, brunch, or as a delicious snack. The addition of pure maple syrup adds a natural sweetness and depth of flavor that complements the banana beautifully. It's sure to become a favorite in your baking repertoire!

**Maple Cranberry Sauce**

Ingredients:

- 12 ounces fresh cranberries (about 3 cups)
- 3/4 cup pure maple syrup
- 1/4 cup water
- 1/2 teaspoon orange zest (optional)
- 1 cinnamon stick (optional)
- Pinch of salt

Instructions:

1. Combine ingredients in a saucepan:
   - In a medium saucepan, combine the fresh cranberries, pure maple syrup, water, orange zest (if using), cinnamon stick (if using), and a pinch of salt.
2. Cook cranberries:
   - Bring the mixture to a boil over medium-high heat.
   - Reduce the heat to medium-low and let the cranberry sauce simmer, stirring occasionally, for about 10-15 minutes. The cranberries will burst and the sauce will thicken.
3. Adjust sweetness:
   - Taste the cranberry sauce and adjust sweetness as desired by adding more maple syrup, if needed.
4. Cool and serve:
   - Remove the saucepan from heat and discard the cinnamon stick (if used).
   - Let the maple cranberry sauce cool to room temperature. It will continue to thicken as it cools.
5. Serve or store:
   - Transfer the maple cranberry sauce to a serving bowl.
   - Serve the sauce chilled or at room temperature alongside your favorite holiday dishes.
6. Enjoy:
   - Enjoy the sweet and tangy flavors of maple cranberry sauce with roasted turkey, chicken, or as a delicious topping for sandwiches and leftovers.

This maple cranberry sauce is a wonderful addition to your Thanksgiving or holiday table, adding a touch of sweetness and depth of flavor that complements savory dishes perfectly. It's easy to make and can be prepared ahead of time, making it a convenient side dish for festive gatherings.

**Maple Sourdough Bread**

Ingredients:

For the sourdough starter:

- 1/2 cup active sourdough starter (100% hydration)
- 1 cup bread flour
- 1/2 cup water

For the bread dough:

- 3 cups bread flour
- 1 cup whole wheat flour (or use additional bread flour)
- 1 1/4 cups water
- 1/4 cup pure maple syrup
- 1 1/2 teaspoons salt

Instructions:

Day 1: Prepare the sourdough starter

1. In a medium bowl, mix together 1/2 cup active sourdough starter, 1 cup bread flour, and 1/2 cup water until well combined. Cover loosely and let it sit at room temperature for 4-6 hours, until bubbly and active.

Day 1: Make the dough

1. In a large mixing bowl, combine 3 cups bread flour, 1 cup whole wheat flour (or additional bread flour), and 1 1/4 cups water. Mix until all the flour is hydrated, cover, and let it rest for 30-60 minutes (autolyse).
2. After the autolyse, add the active sourdough starter from Step 1, 1/4 cup pure maple syrup, and 1 1/2 teaspoons salt to the dough. Mix until well combined.
3. Knead the dough by hand or with a stand mixer fitted with a dough hook for about 10-15 minutes, until the dough is smooth and elastic.
4. Place the dough in a lightly oiled bowl, cover with plastic wrap or a damp towel, and let it ferment at room temperature for about 4-6 hours. During this time, perform a series of stretch and folds every 30 minutes for the first 2 hours.

Day 2: Shape and bake the bread

1. Transfer the dough onto a lightly floured surface. Shape it into a round or oval loaf, ensuring to create tension on the surface of the dough.
2. Place the shaped dough into a proofing basket or a bowl lined with a floured kitchen towel, seam side up. Cover loosely with plastic wrap or a damp towel and let it proof at

room temperature for 1-2 hours, or until it has increased in size and passes the poke test (a slight indentation remains when poked gently with a finger).
3. About 30 minutes before baking, preheat your oven to 450°F (230°C). Place a Dutch oven or baking pot with a lid in the oven to preheat as well.
4. Once the dough is ready, carefully transfer it to the preheated Dutch oven. Score the top of the dough with a sharp knife or lame.
5. Cover the Dutch oven with the lid and bake for 20 minutes. Then, remove the lid and continue baking for another 20-25 minutes, or until the crust is golden brown and the bread sounds hollow when tapped on the bottom.
6. Remove the bread from the oven and let it cool completely on a wire rack before slicing.
7. Enjoy your homemade maple sourdough bread with butter, jam, or as a side to soups and salads.

This maple sourdough bread recipe yields a flavorful loaf with a hint of sweetness from the maple syrup, complemented by the tanginess of the sourdough fermentation. It's a rewarding baking project that results in a delicious and aromatic bread perfect for any occasion.

**Maple Glazed Chicken Wings**

Ingredients:

- 2 lbs chicken wings, split into flats and drumettes
- Salt and pepper, to taste
- 1/2 cup pure maple syrup
- 1/4 cup soy sauce (or tamari for gluten-free)
- 2 tablespoons Dijon mustard
- 2 cloves garlic, minced
- 1 tablespoon apple cider vinegar
- 1/2 teaspoon smoked paprika (optional)
- Chopped fresh parsley or green onions, for garnish (optional)
- Sesame seeds, for garnish (optional)

Instructions:

1. Preheat oven:
    - Preheat your oven to 400°F (200°C). Line a baking sheet with aluminum foil and place a wire rack on top. This helps elevate the wings and allows for even cooking.
2. Prepare the chicken wings:
    - Pat dry the chicken wings with paper towels. Season them generously with salt and pepper.
3. Bake the chicken wings:
    - Arrange the seasoned chicken wings on the wire rack in a single layer.
    - Bake in the preheated oven for 35-40 minutes, or until the wings are golden brown and crispy, turning halfway through cooking.
4. Make the maple glaze:
    - While the wings are baking, prepare the maple glaze. In a small saucepan, combine the pure maple syrup, soy sauce (or tamari), Dijon mustard, minced garlic, apple cider vinegar, and smoked paprika (if using).
    - Bring the mixture to a simmer over medium heat. Cook for 5-7 minutes, stirring occasionally, until the glaze thickens slightly and coats the back of a spoon.
5. Glaze the chicken wings:
    - Once the chicken wings are cooked through and crispy, remove them from the oven.
    - Brush or drizzle the maple glaze generously over the chicken wings, making sure they are evenly coated.
6. Broil (optional):
    - Turn on the broiler setting in your oven. Return the glazed wings to the oven and broil for 2-3 minutes, or until the glaze caramelizes and becomes sticky. Watch closely to prevent burning.
7. Serve:

- Remove the maple glazed chicken wings from the oven. Garnish with chopped fresh parsley or green onions and sesame seeds, if desired.
- Serve immediately as an appetizer or main dish, with extra maple glaze on the side for dipping.

These maple glazed chicken wings are perfect for parties, game day snacks, or any occasion where you want to impress with a deliciously sticky and flavorful dish. The combination of maple syrup, soy sauce, and mustard creates a sweet and savory balance that enhances the natural taste of the chicken wings. Enjoy the sticky goodness!

**Maple Chocolate Truffles**

Ingredients:

- 8 ounces dark chocolate, finely chopped
- 1/2 cup heavy cream
- 2 tablespoons unsalted butter, softened
- 2 tablespoons pure maple syrup
- 1/2 teaspoon vanilla extract
- Cocoa powder, powdered sugar, or finely chopped nuts for coating (optional)

Instructions:

1. Prepare the chocolate:
    - Place the finely chopped dark chocolate in a heatproof bowl.
2. Heat the cream:
    - In a small saucepan, heat the heavy cream over medium heat until it just begins to simmer.
3. Make the ganache:
    - Pour the hot cream over the chopped chocolate. Let it sit undisturbed for 1-2 minutes to soften the chocolate.
    - Gently stir the mixture with a spatula or whisk until the chocolate is completely melted and smooth.
4. Add butter, maple syrup, and vanilla:
    - Stir in the softened butter, pure maple syrup, and vanilla extract until well combined and smooth.
5. Chill the ganache:
    - Cover the bowl with plastic wrap, pressing it directly onto the surface of the chocolate ganache to prevent a skin from forming.
    - Refrigerate the ganache for at least 2 hours, or until firm enough to scoop and roll into balls.
6. Shape the truffles:
    - Once the ganache is chilled and firm, use a spoon or a small cookie scoop to portion out balls of ganache.
    - Roll each portion between your palms to form smooth balls. Place the rolled truffles on a parchment-lined baking sheet.
7. Coat the truffles (optional):
    - Roll the truffles in cocoa powder, powdered sugar, or finely chopped nuts to coat them evenly. This step is optional but adds a nice finish and texture.
8. Chill the truffles:
    - Place the coated truffles back in the refrigerator for about 15-30 minutes to set.
9. Serve and enjoy:
    - Arrange the maple chocolate truffles on a serving platter or in candy cups.
    - Serve at room temperature and enjoy the rich, creamy indulgence of these maple chocolate truffles!

These maple chocolate truffles make a delightful homemade gift or a luxurious treat for any occasion. The combination of dark chocolate and maple syrup creates a flavor profile that is both sophisticated and satisfying. Enjoy these decadent truffles as a special dessert or a thoughtful gift for friends and family!

**Maple Whipped Cream**

Ingredients:

- 1 cup cold heavy cream
- 2-3 tablespoons pure maple syrup (adjust to taste)
- 1/2 teaspoon vanilla extract (optional)

Instructions:

1. Chill equipment:
    - Place a mixing bowl and beaters or whisk attachment from your electric mixer in the refrigerator for at least 10-15 minutes to chill.
2. Whip the cream:
    - Pour the cold heavy cream into the chilled mixing bowl.
    - Using a hand mixer or a stand mixer fitted with the whisk attachment, beat the cream on medium-high speed until soft peaks form. This usually takes about 2-3 minutes.
3. Add maple syrup:
    - Gradually add 2 tablespoons of pure maple syrup while continuing to beat the cream.
    - Taste the whipped cream and add an additional tablespoon of maple syrup if you desire a sweeter flavor.
4. Add vanilla extract (optional):
    - If using, add 1/2 teaspoon of vanilla extract to the whipped cream and beat until incorporated.
5. Beat to stiff peaks:
    - Continue beating the whipped cream until it reaches stiff peaks. This means when you lift the beaters or whisk, the peaks stand up straight without collapsing.
6. Serve:
    - Use immediately to top your favorite desserts or beverages.
7. Store:
    - If you have leftovers, store the maple whipped cream in an airtight container in the refrigerator for up to 24 hours. Before serving again, briefly whisk by hand to restore its fluffy texture.

Maple whipped cream adds a lovely sweetness and subtle maple flavor to desserts, enhancing their overall appeal. It's a versatile topping that pairs well with many treats and is sure to be a hit with maple syrup enthusiasts!

**Maple Brie Appetizers**

Ingredients:

- 1 wheel of Brie cheese (about 8 ounces)
- 1/4 cup pure maple syrup
- 1/4 cup chopped pecans or walnuts (optional)
- Crackers, baguette slices, or apple slices, for serving

Instructions:

1. Preheat oven:
    - Preheat your oven to 350°F (175°C).
2. Prepare the Brie:
    - Place the wheel of Brie cheese on a parchment-lined baking sheet.
3. Score the top of the Brie:
    - Using a sharp knife, lightly score the top rind of the Brie cheese in a crosshatch pattern. This helps the cheese to melt evenly.
4. Drizzle with maple syrup:
    - Drizzle the pure maple syrup evenly over the top of the scored Brie cheese.
5. Add nuts (optional):
    - If using, sprinkle the chopped pecans or walnuts over the maple syrup-covered Brie cheese. This adds a delightful crunch and complements the flavors.
6. Bake the Brie:
    - Bake the Brie cheese in the preheated oven for 10-12 minutes, or until the cheese is softened and gooey inside.
7. Serve:
    - Remove the baked maple Brie from the oven and let it cool for a few minutes.
    - Transfer the warm maple Brie onto a serving platter. Serve immediately with crackers, baguette slices, or apple slices for dipping.
8. Enjoy:
    - Enjoy these delicious maple Brie appetizers as a savory-sweet treat for parties, gatherings, or as a special appetizer before a meal.

This maple Brie appetizer is easy to prepare and impressively tasty, making it a perfect choice for entertaining guests or enjoying a cozy evening at home. The combination of creamy Brie and sweet maple syrup is sure to be a hit!

# Maple Pork Tenderloin

Ingredients:

- 2 pork tenderloins (about 1 pound each)
- Salt and pepper, to taste
- 1/4 cup pure maple syrup
- 2 tablespoons soy sauce (or tamari for gluten-free option)
- 2 tablespoons Dijon mustard
- 2 cloves garlic, minced
- 1 tablespoon olive oil or vegetable oil

Instructions:

1. Prepare the marinade:
    - In a small bowl, whisk together the pure maple syrup, soy sauce, Dijon mustard, minced garlic, salt, and pepper.
2. Marinate the pork:
    - Place the pork tenderloins in a shallow dish or a resealable plastic bag. Pour the maple syrup mixture over the pork, making sure it is well coated.
    - Marinate in the refrigerator for at least 30 minutes, or up to 4 hours. The longer you marinate, the more flavor the pork will absorb.
3. Preheat the oven:
    - Preheat your oven to 400°F (200°C).
4. Sear the pork:
    - Heat olive oil in a large oven-safe skillet over medium-high heat.
    - Remove the pork tenderloins from the marinade, reserving the marinade for later use. Sear the pork tenderloins in the hot skillet until browned on all sides, about 2-3 minutes per side.
5. Roast the pork:
    - Transfer the skillet with the seared pork tenderloins to the preheated oven.
    - Roast for 15-20 minutes, or until the internal temperature reaches 145°F (63°C) for medium rare or 160°F (71°C) for medium, basting occasionally with the reserved marinade.
6. Rest and slice:
    - Remove the pork tenderloins from the oven and transfer them to a cutting board. Cover loosely with foil and let them rest for 5-10 minutes before slicing.
7. Serve:
    - Slice the maple pork tenderloin into medallions and serve warm, drizzling any remaining pan juices over the slices.
8. Enjoy:
    - Enjoy your maple pork tenderloin with your favorite sides such as roasted vegetables, rice, or salad.

This maple pork tenderloin recipe is perfect for a special dinner or holiday meal, combining the savory richness of pork with the sweet and tangy flavors of maple syrup and mustard. It's easy to prepare and sure to impress your guests or family!

**Maple Glazed Brussels Sprouts**

Ingredients:

- 1 lb Brussels sprouts, trimmed and halved
- 2 tablespoons olive oil
- Salt and pepper, to taste
- 2-3 tablespoons pure maple syrup
- 1-2 tablespoons balsamic vinegar (optional, for extra flavor)
- 1/4 cup chopped pecans or walnuts (optional, for crunch)

Instructions:

1. Preheat oven:
    - Preheat your oven to 400°F (200°C).
2. Prepare Brussels sprouts:
    - Trim the ends of the Brussels sprouts and cut them in half lengthwise. Remove any outer leaves that are yellow or wilted.
3. Toss with olive oil and seasonings:
    - In a large bowl, toss the halved Brussels sprouts with olive oil, salt, and pepper until evenly coated.
4. Roast Brussels sprouts:
    - Arrange the Brussels sprouts in a single layer on a baking sheet lined with parchment paper or aluminum foil.
    - Roast in the preheated oven for 20-25 minutes, stirring halfway through, until the Brussels sprouts are tender and caramelized.
5. Make the maple glaze:
    - In a small saucepan, heat the maple syrup over medium heat until it starts to bubble.
    - Reduce the heat to low and simmer for 1-2 minutes, stirring occasionally, until the maple syrup thickens slightly.
6. Glaze the Brussels sprouts:
    - Remove the roasted Brussels sprouts from the oven and transfer them to a serving bowl or dish.
    - Drizzle the warm maple syrup over the roasted Brussels sprouts. Add balsamic vinegar if using, and toss gently to coat evenly.
7. Optional: Add nuts for crunch
    - If desired, sprinkle chopped pecans or walnuts over the maple glazed Brussels sprouts for added crunch and texture.
8. Serve:
    - Serve the maple glazed Brussels sprouts immediately as a side dish or appetizer.
9. Enjoy:
    - Enjoy the sweet and savory flavors of maple glazed Brussels sprouts as a delicious accompaniment to your favorite meals!

This recipe for maple glazed Brussels sprouts is simple yet flavorful, making it a perfect addition to your holiday table or weeknight dinner rotation. The combination of roasted Brussels sprouts with the sticky sweetness of maple syrup is sure to please both kids and adults alike!

**Maple Caramel Corn**

Ingredients:

- 8 cups popped popcorn (about 1/2 cup unpopped kernels)
- 1 cup packed brown sugar
- 1/2 cup unsalted butter
- 1/4 cup pure maple syrup
- 1/4 teaspoon salt
- 1/4 teaspoon baking soda
- 1/2 teaspoon vanilla extract

Instructions:

1. Preheat oven and prepare popcorn:
    - Preheat your oven to 250°F (120°C). Line a large baking sheet with parchment paper or a silicone baking mat.
    - Spread the popped popcorn evenly on the prepared baking sheet. Remove any unpopped kernels.
2. Make the maple caramel sauce:
    - In a medium saucepan, melt the butter over medium heat.
    - Stir in the brown sugar, pure maple syrup, and salt. Cook, stirring constantly, until the mixture comes to a boil.
    - Once boiling, let it cook without stirring for 4-5 minutes to allow it to reach the soft ball stage (about 235°F or 118°C on a candy thermometer).
    - Remove the saucepan from heat and carefully stir in the baking soda and vanilla extract. The mixture will bubble up, so be cautious.
3. Coat the popcorn:
    - Immediately pour the hot maple caramel sauce over the popcorn. Use a spatula or wooden spoon to gently toss and coat the popcorn evenly with the caramel sauce.
4. Bake the caramel corn:
    - Place the baking sheet in the preheated oven and bake for 45-60 minutes, stirring every 15 minutes to ensure even coating and prevent burning.
5. Cool and break apart:
    - Remove the maple caramel corn from the oven and let it cool completely on the baking sheet. It will continue to crisp up as it cools.
6. Serve and store:
    - Once cooled, break the maple caramel corn into clusters and serve immediately.
    - Store any leftovers in an airtight container at room temperature for up to 1 week. Enjoy as a sweet snack or dessert treat!

This maple caramel corn recipe yields a crunchy and addictive snack that balances the sweetness of maple syrup with the buttery caramel coating. It's perfect for parties, movie nights, or as a homemade gift for friends and family. Enjoy the delicious flavors of maple syrup infused into classic caramel corn!

**Maple Mushroom Risotto**

Ingredients:

- 1 cup Arborio rice
- 4 cups vegetable or chicken broth (low-sodium)
- 1/2 cup dry white wine (optional)
- 2 tablespoons olive oil
- 1 tablespoon unsalted butter
- 1 small onion, finely chopped
- 2 cloves garlic, minced
- 8 ounces mushrooms (such as cremini or shiitake), sliced
- 1/4 cup grated Parmesan cheese
- 2 tablespoons pure maple syrup
- Salt and pepper, to taste
- Fresh parsley, chopped, for garnish (optional)

Instructions:

1. Prepare the broth:
   - In a medium saucepan, heat the vegetable or chicken broth over low heat. Keep it warm throughout the cooking process.
2. Sauté the mushrooms:
   - In a large skillet or Dutch oven, heat 1 tablespoon of olive oil over medium heat.
   - Add the sliced mushrooms and cook until they are golden brown and caramelized, about 5-7 minutes. Season with salt and pepper to taste.
   - Remove the mushrooms from the skillet and set aside.
3. Cook the onions and garlic:
   - In the same skillet, add the remaining 1 tablespoon of olive oil and 1 tablespoon of butter.
   - Add the finely chopped onion and sauté until translucent, about 3-4 minutes.
   - Stir in the minced garlic and cook for another 1 minute until fragrant.
4. Toast the rice:
   - Add the Arborio rice to the skillet with the onions and garlic. Cook, stirring constantly, for 1-2 minutes until the rice is lightly toasted and coated with oil.
5. Deglaze with wine (optional):
   - If using wine, pour the white wine into the skillet with the rice. Cook, stirring constantly, until the wine is absorbed.
6. Add the broth:
   - Begin adding the warm broth to the skillet, one ladleful at a time, stirring frequently. Allow each addition of broth to be absorbed by the rice before adding the next ladleful.
   - Continue cooking and stirring the risotto for about 20-25 minutes, or until the rice is creamy and tender but still slightly firm (al dente). You may not need to use all of the broth.

7. Finish the risotto:
    - Stir in the cooked mushrooms, grated Parmesan cheese, and pure maple syrup. Taste and adjust seasoning with salt and pepper as needed.
8. Serve:
    - Divide the maple mushroom risotto among serving plates or bowls.
    - Garnish with chopped fresh parsley if desired, and serve immediately while hot.

This maple mushroom risotto recipe serves as a delicious main dish or a hearty side. The combination of savory mushrooms with the sweetness of maple syrup adds depth and complexity to this classic Italian rice dish. Enjoy the comforting flavors of maple mushroom risotto with family and friends!

## Maple Bourbon BBQ Sauce

Ingredients:

- 1 cup ketchup
- 1/2 cup apple cider vinegar
- 1/4 cup pure maple syrup
- 1/4 cup bourbon whiskey
- 2 tablespoons Worcestershire sauce
- 2 tablespoons Dijon mustard
- 2 cloves garlic, minced
- 1 teaspoon smoked paprika
- 1/2 teaspoon onion powder
- 1/2 teaspoon garlic powder
- 1/2 teaspoon salt
- 1/4 teaspoon black pepper

Instructions:

1. Combine ingredients:
    - In a medium saucepan, combine the ketchup, apple cider vinegar, maple syrup, bourbon whiskey, Worcestershire sauce, Dijon mustard, minced garlic, smoked paprika, onion powder, garlic powder, salt, and black pepper.
2. Simmer:
    - Bring the mixture to a simmer over medium heat, stirring occasionally to combine all the ingredients.
3. Reduce heat and cook:
    - Reduce the heat to low and let the sauce simmer gently for 15-20 minutes, stirring occasionally, until it thickens to your desired consistency.
4. Adjust seasoning:
    - Taste the sauce and adjust the seasoning if needed. You can add more salt, pepper, or maple syrup to adjust the sweetness.
5. Cool and store:
    - Remove the maple bourbon BBQ sauce from heat and let it cool slightly.
    - Transfer the sauce to a glass jar or airtight container and refrigerate until ready to use. The flavors will develop more if you let it sit for a few hours or overnight.
6. Serve:
    - Use maple bourbon BBQ sauce as a marinade for chicken, pork, or beef before grilling or baking.
    - Brush it on grilled meats during the last few minutes of cooking for a sticky glaze.
    - Serve it as a dipping sauce for chicken tenders, fries, or as a condiment for burgers and sandwiches.

This maple bourbon BBQ sauce recipe yields a flavorful and versatile sauce that adds a unique twist to your favorite barbecue dishes. The combination of maple syrup and bourbon whiskey creates a sweet and smoky profile that pairs perfectly with grilled meats and vegetables. Enjoy experimenting with this delicious sauce in your cooking!

**Maple Apple Butter**

Ingredients:

- 6-8 medium-sized apples (such as Granny Smith or Honeycrisp), peeled, cored, and sliced
- 1/2 cup pure maple syrup
- 1/2 cup apple cider or apple juice
- 1 teaspoon ground cinnamon
- 1/4 teaspoon ground nutmeg
- 1/4 teaspoon ground cloves
- Pinch of salt

Instructions:

1. Prepare the apples:
    - Peel, core, and slice the apples. It's important to have even-sized pieces so they cook evenly.
2. Cook the apples:
    - In a large pot or Dutch oven, combine the sliced apples, maple syrup, apple cider (or juice), ground cinnamon, ground nutmeg, ground cloves, and a pinch of salt.
    - Bring the mixture to a boil over medium-high heat, then reduce the heat to low.
    - Simmer, uncovered, stirring occasionally, for about 30-40 minutes or until the apples are very soft and starting to break down.
3. Blend or mash the apples:
    - Once the apples are cooked and soft, you have two options:
    a) Use an immersion blender directly in the pot to blend the mixture until smooth.
    b) Transfer the mixture to a blender or food processor and blend until smooth. Be careful when blending hot liquids.
4. Cook down to desired consistency:
    - Return the blended mixture to the pot if you transferred it for blending.
    - Cook over low heat, stirring frequently, until the mixture thickens to a spreadable consistency. This can take 1-2 hours depending on how thick you prefer your apple butter.
5. Adjust sweetness and seasoning:
    - Taste the maple apple butter and adjust sweetness by adding more maple syrup if desired.
    - If the flavors need more spice, you can add a bit more cinnamon, nutmeg, or cloves.
6. Cool and store:
    - Once cooked to your liking, remove the maple apple butter from heat and let it cool completely.

- - Transfer to clean, sterilized jars or airtight containers. Store in the refrigerator for up to 2-3 weeks.
7. Serve:
    - Enjoy your homemade maple apple butter on toast, pancakes, waffles, biscuits, or as a filling in pastries.

Maple apple butter is a delicious way to preserve the flavors of apples with a hint of maple sweetness. It's a versatile spread that can be enjoyed throughout the year and makes a wonderful homemade gift during the fall season.

**Maple Rum Cake**

Ingredients:

*For the cake:*

- 1 cup unsalted butter, softened
- 1 cup granulated sugar
- 4 large eggs
- 2 teaspoons vanilla extract
- 1/2 cup pure maple syrup
- 1/2 cup dark rum
- 2 cups all-purpose flour
- 1 teaspoon baking powder
- 1/2 teaspoon baking soda
- 1/2 teaspoon salt
- 1/2 cup sour cream

*For the maple rum glaze:*

- 1/4 cup unsalted butter
- 1/4 cup pure maple syrup
- 1/4 cup dark rum
- 1/2 cup powdered sugar

Instructions:

1. Preheat oven and prepare pan:
    - Preheat your oven to 350°F (175°C). Grease and flour a 10-inch Bundt pan or a 9x13-inch baking pan.
2. Make the cake:
    - In a large bowl, cream together the softened butter and granulated sugar until light and fluffy.
    - Add the eggs, one at a time, beating well after each addition. Stir in the vanilla extract.
    - Gradually add the maple syrup and dark rum, mixing until well combined.
    - In a separate bowl, whisk together the flour, baking powder, baking soda, and salt.
    - Gradually add the dry ingredients to the wet ingredients, alternating with the sour cream, beginning and ending with the flour mixture. Mix until just combined.
3. Bake the cake:
    - Pour the batter into the prepared pan and spread it evenly.
    - Bake in the preheated oven for 40-45 minutes (for Bundt pan) or 30-35 minutes (for 9x13-inch pan), or until a toothpick inserted into the center comes out clean.
4. Make the maple rum glaze:

        - In a small saucepan, melt the butter over medium heat. Stir in the maple syrup and dark rum.
        - Bring the mixture to a gentle boil, then remove from heat and let it cool slightly.
        - Whisk in the powdered sugar until smooth and well combined.
5. Finish the cake:
        - Once the cake is baked, remove it from the oven and let it cool in the pan for 10 minutes.
        - Invert the cake onto a wire rack placed over a baking sheet or parchment paper.
        - While the cake is still warm, brush or drizzle the maple rum glaze over the top and sides of the cake, allowing it to soak in.
6. Serve:
        - Allow the cake to cool completely before slicing and serving.
7. Enjoy:
        - Serve your maple rum cake slices with a dollop of whipped cream or a scoop of vanilla ice cream, if desired.

This maple rum cake is moist, flavorful, and perfect for special occasions or as a comforting dessert during cooler months. The combination of maple syrup and rum adds a delicious depth of flavor that will impress your guests and delight your taste buds!

**Maple Glazed Carrot Cake**

Ingredients:

*For the carrot cake:*

- 2 cups all-purpose flour
- 1 teaspoon baking powder
- 1 teaspoon baking soda
- 1/2 teaspoon salt
- 1 teaspoon ground cinnamon
- 1/2 teaspoon ground nutmeg
- 1/2 teaspoon ground ginger
- 1 cup granulated sugar
- 1 cup brown sugar, packed
- 1 cup vegetable oil or melted coconut oil
- 4 large eggs
- 1 teaspoon vanilla extract
- 2 cups grated carrots (about 3-4 medium carrots)
- 1/2 cup crushed pineapple, drained
- 1/2 cup chopped walnuts or pecans (optional)

*For the maple glaze:*

- 1/4 cup unsalted butter
- 1/4 cup pure maple syrup
- 1 cup powdered sugar
- 1-2 tablespoons milk or cream, as needed

Instructions:

1. Preheat oven and prepare pan:
    - Preheat your oven to 350°F (175°C). Grease and flour a 9x13-inch baking pan or two 9-inch round cake pans.
2. Make the carrot cake:
    - In a large bowl, whisk together the flour, baking powder, baking soda, salt, cinnamon, nutmeg, and ginger.
    - In another large bowl, combine the granulated sugar, brown sugar, and oil. Mix until well combined.
    - Add the eggs, one at a time, mixing well after each addition. Stir in the vanilla extract.
    - Gradually add the dry ingredients to the wet ingredients, mixing until just combined.
    - Fold in the grated carrots, crushed pineapple, and chopped nuts (if using), until evenly distributed.

3. Bake the cake:
   - Pour the batter into the prepared baking pan(s), spreading it evenly.
   - Bake in the preheated oven for 30-35 minutes (for a 9x13-inch pan) or 25-30 minutes (for round pans), or until a toothpick inserted into the center comes out clean.
4. Cool the cake:
   - Remove the cake from the oven and let it cool in the pan for 10 minutes.
   - Transfer the cake onto a wire rack to cool completely before glazing.
5. Make the maple glaze:
   - In a small saucepan, melt the butter over medium heat. Stir in the maple syrup until combined.
   - Remove the saucepan from heat and gradually whisk in the powdered sugar until smooth.
   - If the glaze is too thick, stir in milk or cream, 1 tablespoon at a time, until desired consistency is reached.
6. Glaze the cake:
   - Once the cake has cooled completely, pour or drizzle the maple glaze over the top of the cake, spreading it evenly with a spatula if necessary.
7. Serve:
   - Slice and serve your maple glazed carrot cake. Optionally, garnish with additional chopped nuts or a sprinkle of cinnamon.
8. Enjoy:
   - Enjoy this moist and flavorful maple glazed carrot cake with its delicious blend of spices and the added sweetness of the maple glaze. It's perfect for any occasion or as a special treat!

This maple glazed carrot cake recipe will surely be a hit with its tender crumb, moist texture, and delightful maple syrup flavor. It's a wonderful dessert to share with family and friends!

**Maple Coconut Macaroons**

Ingredients:

- 3 cups shredded sweetened coconut
- 1/2 cup pure maple syrup
- 2 large egg whites
- 1/4 teaspoon salt
- 1/2 teaspoon vanilla extract

Instructions:

1. Preheat oven:
    - Preheat your oven to 325°F (160°C). Line a baking sheet with parchment paper or a silicone baking mat.
2. Mix ingredients:
    - In a mixing bowl, combine the shredded coconut, pure maple syrup, salt, and vanilla extract. Mix well until all the coconut is coated evenly with the maple syrup.
3. Whip egg whites:
    - In a separate bowl, beat the egg whites until stiff peaks form. This can be done with a hand mixer or stand mixer.
4. Combine ingredients:
    - Gently fold the whipped egg whites into the coconut mixture until well combined. Be careful not to deflate the egg whites too much.
5. Form macaroons:
    - Using a spoon or cookie scoop, scoop out about 2 tablespoons of the coconut mixture and drop it onto the prepared baking sheet, spacing them about 1 inch apart.
6. Bake:
    - Bake in the preheated oven for 20-25 minutes, or until the tops of the macaroons are golden brown.
7. Cool:
    - Remove from the oven and let the macaroons cool on the baking sheet for 5 minutes.
8. Serve:
    - Transfer the maple coconut macaroons to a wire rack to cool completely.
9. Enjoy:
    - Once cooled, enjoy your maple coconut macaroons as a delicious treat with a cup of tea or coffee.

These maple coconut macaroons are naturally gluten-free and have a wonderful combination of flavors from the maple syrup and coconut. They make a perfect dessert for parties, holidays, or any time you crave a sweet treat with a hint of maple sweetness.

**Maple Espresso Brownies**

Ingredients:

- 1/2 cup unsalted butter
- 1 cup granulated sugar
- 1/2 cup cocoa powder
- 2 teaspoons instant espresso powder (or instant coffee)
- 1/4 teaspoon salt
- 1 teaspoon vanilla extract
- 2 large eggs
- 1/2 cup all-purpose flour
- 1/4 cup pure maple syrup

Instructions:

1. Preheat oven and prepare baking pan:
    - Preheat your oven to 350°F (175°C). Grease or line an 8x8-inch baking pan with parchment paper.
2. Melt butter and sugar:
    - In a medium saucepan, melt the butter over medium heat. Once melted, remove from heat and stir in the granulated sugar until well combined.
3. Add cocoa powder and espresso powder:
    - Stir in the cocoa powder and instant espresso powder (or instant coffee) until smooth and well incorporated.
4. Mix in salt, vanilla, and eggs:
    - Add the salt and vanilla extract to the chocolate mixture. Mix well.
    - Add the eggs, one at a time, mixing well after each addition until the mixture is smooth.
5. Fold in flour:
    - Gradually add the flour to the batter, stirring until just combined. Be careful not to overmix.
6. Add maple syrup:
    - Pour the pure maple syrup into the batter and gently fold it in until it's evenly distributed.
7. Bake:
    - Pour the brownie batter into the prepared baking pan and spread it out evenly.
    - Bake in the preheated oven for 25-30 minutes, or until a toothpick inserted into the center comes out with moist crumbs.
8. Cool and slice:
    - Allow the brownies to cool completely in the pan on a wire rack.
    - Once cooled, lift the brownies out of the pan using the parchment paper and cut into squares.
9. Serve and enjoy:

- Serve the maple espresso brownies as is or with a scoop of vanilla ice cream for a delicious dessert.

These maple espresso brownies are rich, fudgy, and have a delightful hint of espresso and maple syrup flavors. They're perfect for chocolate lovers and coffee enthusiasts alike!

**Maple Creme Brulee**

Ingredients:

- 2 cups heavy cream
- 1/2 cup pure maple syrup
- 6 large egg yolks
- 1 teaspoon vanilla extract
- Pinch of salt
- Granulated sugar (for caramelizing)

Instructions:

1. Preheat oven:
    - Preheat your oven to 300°F (150°C). Place 6 ramekins (about 4-6 ounces each) in a deep baking dish or roasting pan.
2. Prepare the custard mixture:
    - In a saucepan, heat the heavy cream and maple syrup over medium heat until it just begins to simmer. Stir occasionally to ensure the mixture does not scorch.
3. Whisk egg yolks:
    - In a separate bowl, whisk the egg yolks until smooth.
4. Temper the eggs:
    - Gradually pour the hot cream mixture into the egg yolks, whisking constantly, to temper the eggs. This prevents them from scrambling.
5. Add vanilla and salt:
    - Stir in the vanilla extract and a pinch of salt, mixing until well combined.
6. Strain the mixture:
    - Strain the custard mixture through a fine-mesh sieve into a clean bowl or pitcher. This helps remove any lumps or egg solids for a smooth texture.
7. Pour into ramekins:
    - Divide the custard mixture evenly among the ramekins placed in the baking dish.
8. Bake in a water bath:
    - Carefully pour hot water into the baking dish, around the ramekins, until it reaches about halfway up the sides of the ramekins. This creates a water bath.
    - Bake in the preheated oven for 30-35 minutes, or until the edges are set but the center of each crème brûlée still jiggles slightly when shaken.
9. Chill:
    - Remove the ramekins from the water bath and let them cool to room temperature.
    - Cover each ramekin with plastic wrap and refrigerate for at least 4 hours, or preferably overnight, to set and chill thoroughly.
10. Caramelize the sugar:
    - Just before serving, sprinkle a thin, even layer of granulated sugar over the top of each chilled crème brûlée.

- Use a kitchen torch to caramelize the sugar until it melts and forms a golden-brown crust. Alternatively, place the ramekins under a broiler for 1-2 minutes, watching carefully to avoid burning.
11. Serve and enjoy:
    - Let the caramelized sugar harden for a few minutes before serving your maple crème brûlée.
    - Enjoy the creamy, rich texture and the delightful combination of flavors from the maple syrup and vanilla.

This maple crème brûlée recipe yields a luxurious dessert with a silky smooth custard and a crunchy caramelized sugar topping. It's perfect for special occasions or anytime you want to indulge in a sophisticated treat with a hint of maple sweetness.

www.ingramcontent.com/pod-product-compliance
Lightning Source LLC
LaVergne TN
LVHW081610060526
838201LV00054B/2181